FOCUS ON THEM

BECOME THE MANAGER YOUR PEOPLE NEED YOU TO BE

EDITED BY
RYAN CHANGCOCO
MEGAN COLE
AND JACK HARLOW

atd
PRESS

ATD Press is an internationally renowned source of insightful and practical information on talent development, training, and professional development.

ATD Press
1640 King Street
Alexandria, VA 22314 USA

Ordering information: Books published by ATD Press can be purchased by visiting ATD's website at www.td.org/books or by calling 800.628.2783 or 703.683.8100.

Library of Congress Control Number: 2018962010

ISBN-10: 1-56286-871-3
ISBN-13: 978-1-56286-871-0
e-ISBN: 978-1-56286-972-4

ATD Press Editorial Staff
Director: Kristine Luecker
Manager: Melissa Jones
Community of Practice Manager, Management: Ryan Changcoco
Developmental Editor: Jack Harlow
Text Design: Michelle Jose
Cover Design: Alban Fischer, Alban Fischer Design
Printed by Versa Press Inc., East Peoria, IL

To the ideal manager, may you always strive to be your best self.

Contents

Introduction vii

    1. Accountability 1
    2. Communication 27
    3. Collaboration.. 61
    4. Engagement... 93
    5. Listening and Assessing... 117

Appendix.. 149
Acknowledgments.. 173
References 175
About the Contributors.. 181
About the Editors 185
Index 189

Introduction

"Managing people is easy."
—No one ever

The workplace is changing. Some call it an engagement crisis, and others call it the Millennial takeover. Whatever it is, there's one thing we all know: The management approaches that we once relied on need to evolve to get in front of the ever-changing workplace. Clearly, it's time to switch up our approach to management.

For some of us, the goal is to find new and innovative ways to better engage and retain employees. Whether that means holding people accountable, enhancing communication, or engaging staff, we can all stand to improve our methods. For others, it's about getting back to basics, and that's what this book is all about. At the Association for Talent Development (ATD), we think it's important to improve upon the five basic skills all managers need: accountability, communication, collaboration, engagement, and listening and assessing.

Great Managers Make Connections; Bad Managers . . .

Great managers are few and far between. When we came together to edit this book, we immediately began to think about the truly great managers we've had. For Ryan it's Ed, his boss at a previous stop. Together, they worked on the federal side for a healthcare insurance company. At the time, the team's function was brand-new, and Ed had a limited amount of experience with the job he was brought in to do; he'd never managed the kind of product that they were tasked with developing. Even so, Ed quickly became a memorable manager with a management style that was trusting, supportive, and transparent.

He used to say, "Work is just one part of life; never forget what the truly important things are to you." At that moment, Ed connected with Ryan and his other direct reports as people—it was clear that they were more than just cogs he needed to keep the business running. As their work continued, Ed felt pressure from the top to ensure they were performing, and performing well. He and Ryan had many conversations about what was going on, not just to commiserate but to foster an open and honest environment and help Ryan understand the decisions Ed had to make. Ryan found these conversations refreshing, and they cultivated a deeper sense of trust.

Unfortunately, not all managers are great, which is why we're bringing this book to you. It's more likely that you've come into contact with a bad manager. In fact, most people can come up with many more stories about bad managers than they can good—there's simply no shortage of bad managers.

Having a bad boss can make an otherwise decent job quickly lose its appeal. There are myriad types of bad bosses, too: The micromanager. The steam roller. The blame shifter. And they wreak havoc on engagement, productivity, and performance. When people like their boss, they ramp up their productivity, become happier on the job, and maintain a better work-life balance. Alternatively, when employees don't like their boss, they are more likely to leave.

But what about managers who don't develop their employees? Sometimes managers may seem fine at face value, but don't do much in the way of developing their direct reports. Nearly every expert on employee engagement agrees there is a single, most impactful means of increasing employee engagement and performance: the manager. Developing employees is a big part of a manager's responsibilities, so why are some managers so bad at it?

The Accidental Manager

Accidental managers are everywhere. Often, the manager was an individual contributor at the top of their game who was promoted either because the organization didn't want to lose them or because it seemed like the natural progression. But once they become a manager, it's a whole different story. A stellar individual contributor doesn't necessarily translate into an effective manager. Indeed, most companies fail to prepare their employees as they transition into management. When a new manager transitions into the role from an individual contributor position, it becomes less about the work, and more about the people. Less about the "me" and more about the "we."

Not only is a lack of training and preparation to blame for lousy managers, but oftentimes people don't know what "good" management even looks like. Consider this: If all you've ever had are bad managers, how would you know what to do when you become a manager? It's likely that you'd emulate what you've seen your entire professional life. While some managers consciously abuse their authority, the vast majority of "bad" managers don't realize that they're underperforming and underserving the people relying on them to lead. Unfortunately, as is often true in business, ignorance excuses naught.

Developing employees comes with the territory when you're a manager. And yet, many managers lack the skills and competence to effectively do this part of the job, and their organizations don't always provide the opportunities to develop them. As such, it's necessary for frontline managers to learn the skills needed, with or without the help of their talent development function.

But which skills will best serve managers in reaching their full potential at developing their employees? This question led ATD to conduct a little management research.

The ACCEL Model

In 2015, ATD Research conducted a poll of learning executives, asking them to identify their top skills related to managerial success. Using that research, ATD developed the ACCEL skills model, which outlines the five key skills managers need: accountability, communication, collaboration, engagement, and listening and assessing.

Shortly after its creation, ATD Research used the model in its report *ACCEL: The Skills That Make a Winning Manager* to examine which skills were necessary to successfully develop a manager's direct reports. This was a natural extension of the model, because developing direct reports is a critical responsibility of the manager role.

The study found that just 46 percent of organizations had identified skills related to managerial success in developing direct reports. Further, a majority of participants indicated that each of the five ACCEL skills contributed to managerial success in developing direct reports, ranging from 75 to 86 percent. Perhaps most surprising was that fewer than a third of respondents indicated that managers at their organization exhibited each of the ACCEL skills when working with their direct reports.

Even though participants believed these five ACCEL skills contributed to managerial success in developing direct reports, they reported that opportunities to cultivate them were relatively rare. Communication was the skill with the largest opportunity for development; 38 percent of respondents said managers were given opportunities to develop communication proficiency to a high or very high extent. Managers were least likely to have the opportunity to develop collaboration skills (30 percent). While these numbers may seem low, consider that manager development isn't a priority for 43 percent of organizations.

Until organizations and talent development departments fill the void of absent or neglected management development programs, managers and their direct reports will be at a disadvantage. Fortunately, you can take steps to improve your ACCEL skills on your own.

The Book

We've assembled some of the best minds in management and talent development to share their knowledge on the skills you need to excel as a manager. Throughout this book, we and our contributors will illustrate how to implement these skills in your life, while offering actionable tips and best practices. Let's go over each of the ACCEL skills in turn.

Accountability

When many managers focus on team accountability, it's often first perceived through the lens of some threat—imposing negative consequences upon a poor performer or implying negative repercussions should a team member not complete their work in a thorough fashion. But this narrow view of accountability—focusing on the negative—can cause fear and become a drain on productivity. The best managers understand that accountability is most effective when team members find motivation within themselves to get their work done.

In the first chapter, ATD Vice President of Content and Digital Marketing Tim Ito introduces FACES, a human-centered approach to accountability that involves focus, apprenticeship, challenge, education, and safety. Managers can instill a culture of accountability within their teams by focusing on organizational goals and day-to-day priorities; offering opportunities to shadow experts and learn continuously; challenging direct reports with meaningful, achievable goals; and ensuring everyone feels safe to succeed and fail.

Communication

Workplace communication no longer occurs just around the watercooler, in meetings, or via email—tasks, responsibilities, and new projects are all discussed in a faster, more informal manner across the organization through emerging technologies. As this information cascades down from manager to direct report, the opportunities for miscommunication skyrocket. That's why, more than ever, a manager who lacks strong communication skills is unlikely to succeed. Managers who don't match words with actions, convey vague versus concrete requests, and shy away from tough conversations will struggle to develop their team.

In his chapter, business communication expert Ken O'Quinn shows how the truly gifted communicators appreciate the power of language and navigate the manager-as-talent-developer dynamic. Only by being transparent and open can managers strengthen their credibility to the point that they can influence their team. This is the foundation that managers need to lay to deliver targeted, actionable feedback. And through this feedback, the manager can communicate the organization's vision, facilitate change, and connect with their employees.

Collaboration

Why, with the ever-increasing means to communicate and connect with one another, does effective collaboration appear to be out of reach for most managers? For starters, a manager needs to create an environment of teamwork before collaboration is even possible. This is a daunting task for new and even seasoned managers when the demand for short-term wins often triumphs over longer-term culture building. Managers who excel in collaboration nurture relationships between all team members, clarify team roles, and encourage cooperation toward achieving a common goal. By encouraging trust and relationship building between team members, managers position direct reports to share knowledge with and learn from one another.

In his chapter, Winsor Jenkins, founder and president of Winsor Jenkins & Associates, provides a clear path to practicing genuine team collaboration. It all begins with shifting your mindset from lecturing to listening, from controlling to influencing, and from valuing likeness to valuing differences. You also need to assess your self-awareness and check your underlying assumptions to determine how you and your team can best collaborate given the available resources, nature of work, and external demands. By assuming the dual roles of manager and coach, you can create a culture of collaboration that allows your direct reports to grow themselves and produce sustainable results: a win-win.

Engagement

Employee engagement leads the priority list of most executives as they search for solutions to attract new talent while retaining their high performers. While engagement is often defined as the act of motivating, inspiring, and involving employees, organizations still grapple with the "how." Increasingly, they're turning to managers, the frontline employee's main organizational touchpoint, to boost engagement. For most managers this is unchartered territory and just one more responsibility added on to making sure the work gets done on time; some continue to elevate meeting the bottom line over driving engagement. But the best managers focus on both, and they do them well.

In her chapter, organization development and inclusion consultant Hunter Haines tackles the questions of what engages employees, why managers have failed to do their part, and how they can fill this essential role. Engaged employees understand their specific role and its importance, and they feel valued and involved in decision making. Managers who engage their direct reports share important organizational information throughout the employee life cycle, not just once at the beginning and then occasionally in annual feedback sessions. The result? Direct reports who are committed to their work and make positive contributions to their own development and the company.

Listening and Assessing

Because organizations rely more and more on managers to maintain organizational productivity, managers have been led to believe that having all the right answers and always knowing what to say is the only way to succeed. Rarely are managers encouraged to sit back, listen, and then assess. And when they do, managers often fall into typical routines: They listen for what they expect to be true, they listen to demonstrate their own expertise, or they listen impatiently and apathetically. But listening is an essential information-gathering, critical-thinking, and processing tool during interactions with direct reports. By not developing listening skills, managers fail to best serve their organization and often make less accurate judgments; too many employees believe their managers do not listen to their concerns.

In her chapter, Michele Nevarez, an executive coach and seasoned HR executive, shows how the ability to listen as a manager is directly linked to team performance, engagement, and quality of work. Naturally, this requires emotional intelligence, recognizing your own and others' emotions, and using emotional information to guide your behavior and assessments. Managers who are skilled at listening and assessing use these abilities to identify areas of strength and improvement in direct reports. In the end, what makes a good listener is also what allows managers to inspire their team to go above and beyond consistently in their work.

Don't Worry, You'll Manage

The reality of it is that becoming a great manager is not easy, nor will it ever be. It takes time, patience, and a willingness to admit when something is not working. And beyond that, managers who aim to improve must genuinely want to and care about their employees.

For those who are embarking on the journey to improving their management skills, the upside is that there are a ton of resources on how to manage well. Blog after blog, Ted Talk after Ted Talk, expert after expert, and book after book (including this one), there are resources everywhere to help with every single facet of management. It is our hope that with this book we have advanced the conversation and provided the tools you need to truly succeed. If you're not sure about where to start, sit back and think about all your own experiences with good (and bad) managers, and go from there.

Just remember that becoming a good manager is an ongoing process. When you think you've perfected it, something new will come up that you don't expect. Don't let this discourage you. Tomorrow is a new day for you to try something new and to learn from yesterday's mistake.

1

Accountability

Timothy Ito

You might say the most important job I ever had was one that no longer exists today—at least not in the same capacity that it used to. In 1993, I started my professional career as a fact-checker for *U.S. News & World Report*. Fact-checking was a serious business—the responsibility of a separate editorial department that made sure the claims and facts stated in a magazine's print edition were true. The *New Yorker* had a famed fact-checking department, as did *National Geographic* and other magazines such as *Time* and *Newsweek*. This was before the Internet, when print magazine subscriptions still ruled the day.

In most places, the profession was a deadline-driven business. Every Friday night, fact-checkers, along with the copy editors, top editors, and writers, "put the magazine to bed," working into the wee hours to send the final copy to the printers. These deadlines often meant working under a lot of pressure; as fact-checkers, we had to verify the accuracy of the sources provided by the writer and do the little things, such as making sure names and places were spelled correctly. We were responsible for confirming any of the details upon which the publication's integrity hung.

Because of the emphasis placed on accuracy and attention to detail, the role proved to be a great training ground for a job as a writer and reporter, which is the path I eventually took. Perhaps the greatest lesson I learned revolved around the importance of accountability. Not just individual accountability in terms of getting work done accurately under a deadline, but more important, the accountability leaders can instill in their team.

Let me give some perspective on this.

When many leaders focus on team accountability, it's often first perceived through the lens of some threat, such as imposing negative consequences upon a poor performer or implying negative repercussions should a team member submit incomplete work or fail to meet a deadline.

That's not necessarily a bad thing. Negative consequences, if applied thoughtfully, can spur team members to finish their work the way a boss wants while also providing a sense of urgency. But when they're the only tool a leader uses, the work atmosphere often becomes draining because team members can see only the downside, rather than the upside, to the work they do. Also, most leaders understand that accountability is best when it's intrinsic and an individual team member is motivated on their own to get the work done and get it right.

That latter approach is what I learned from Kathleen Phillips, my boss at *U.S. News & World Report.* By the time I got there, Kathleen had led the fact-checking department for more than a decade. What made her special was that she had not only knowledge, but the wisdom and energy to spread what she knew to others. The atmosphere she created was unique in the sense that her staff seemed to be intrinsically motivated and accountable for their own results. In fact, much of my own management style today is modeled on her approach.

What made it effective?

FACES: A Human Approach to Accountability

I've often thought about why Kathleen proved to be such a successful manager, particularly around accountability. I believe she understood that accountability, at its heart, is primarily about understanding that people are the center of team effectiveness. Through studying her methods I've come up with a framework of core principles called FACES (focus, apprenticeship, challenge, education, and safety).

First, let's take a step back and look at the big picture. What do you want your team to accomplish? Around what dates? Remember, it's not just getting them to finish the work; it's getting them to finish the right work, the right way, and to prioritize their deliverables because multitasking is the norm in most occupations.

So how do you start approaching accountability? Let's look at a scenario: You're a busy manager who is often in meetings with your boss or your colleagues in other divisions. Your team has to accomplish lots of work, so you delegate task after task to your employees. After you assign the tasks, you expect each one to not only be checked off the list, but also be done well and in a timely manner. When the tasks get done, you believe your employees did well. When they aren't or when they aren't done well, you look at your employees and ask why. You begin to question their ability to get the job done.

It's not uncommon.

But that's a mindset that can get managers into trouble. The responsibility for an employee getting the work done rests not only on the employee but ultimately with you as their manager. And that's where you can start providing the focus they need.

Focus

There are two aspects of focus worth paying attention to. The first involves the broader sense of the word: What's the organization's overall mission? How does the team's work fit into that? What's the group's overall goal? How is it measured? What translates into success?

As a manager, one of your most important roles is to communicate all those things up front to employees. On my first day at *U.S. News & World Report,* Kathleen took me around the building and we discussed the history of the magazine, its legacy, the role it played in covering important events that happened in history, the famed covers, and the editors of what, at that point, was its almost 60-year history.

Although she never said this to me, I think the reason she gave me this history lesson was to provide context for the work we were doing and help us, as fact-checkers, understand that quality and reputation mattered. Kathleen then followed up the tour with a discussion about our role as fact-checkers in the editorial process. We were the guardians of the magazine's legacy, she said. We were the last line of defense against errors that would harm its reputation.

In other words, she provided a clear expression of the role fact-checkers played at the magazine.

And this is where a lot of managers often fail their employees. A 2014 Partners in Leadership accountability study sheds some light on this. According to the survey, "only 15% of organizations have clearly defined, cascaded messages of organizational goals. Specifically, 93% of employees don't understand what their organization is trying to accomplish, 85% of leaders aren't defining what their people should be working on, and 84% of the workforce describes itself as trying but failing or avoiding accountability."

That broader focus provides purpose. And purpose is a large part of what drives employee accountability.

If managers—often due to time constraints or their own lack of understanding about the organization's mission and vision—don't provide that context, their employees won't understand why they're doing what they're doing. How many managerial peers do you know who basically just throw employees into the work and say: "OK, here's your first task"?

After you've communicated the broader picture to employees, the second aspect of focus involves prioritization. Do you know what your employees are working on every day? Do you care? Do you ask them?

They sound like flippant questions, but a lot of managers don't know what their employees are doing on a day-to-day basis. While managers might generally understand their employees' jobs, they often don't communicate which parts of those jobs are the most important.

At *U.S. News & World Report,* Kathleen, as head of the fact-checking department, would divvy up our weekly assignments often based on our backgrounds. I fact-checked a lot of the articles on Asia, simply because I had lived there and knew a little bit about the countries in the region. But she never handed over the files and sources to check without giving us the background or backstory on the piece. This was especially true for new employees. She would make sure to give us the heads-up on the need to check certain articles more thoroughly because of their litigious nature (or because the writer was often sloppy in sourcing). In other words, she told us which articles had priority in terms of making sure things were right.

As you can imagine, if controversial articles had the wrong facts, it could mean disaster for our reputation—inaccuracy in any part of the article would inevitably lead people to question the rest of the article. (Or worse, sue for libel.)

Kathleen's guidance provided focus for what we should be working on and paying attention to. So many times, I've seen managers make that critical mistake—they delegate, but then let the employees dictate what they work on as a way to give them the freedom to be creative and take their own risks. These managers further justify the practice by saying they "don't have time" to deal with knowing what tasks employees are working on.

That's a lousy excuse. And frankly, it's lazy managing. Part of the role of ensuring accountability involves not just delegating responsibility, but also defining the limits of the figurative sandbox in which employees play. If "anything" is fair game, then the work output will often have no relationship to what the business unit or organization is trying to accomplish. Thus, managers need to define those limits and make the effort to understand and prioritize the work that employees do.

But what about creativity? Won't setting limits hinder your employees' ability to develop and create more efficient solutions? Isn't that why managers delegate work? Where is the line between prioritizing employees' work and micromanaging?

Part of the art of management is understanding how to harness an employee's creativity within the scope of the work that they do. Telling them that anything is possible would be neither constructive nor particularly helpful in advancing an organization's cause. But helping them find or giving them the freedom to innovate within a particular area or context is different. In that way, managers can focus employees on solving the issues that are most pressing.

A good example of this is Spotify, a music and multimedia streaming company with roughly 83 million paid subscribers as of this writing (Steigrad 2018). Spotify takes a unique approach to balance employee creativity with accountability. One way the company does this is to develop alignment without excessive control. As Michael Mankins and Eric Garton (2017) note in *Harvard Business Review:* "The central organization feature that shapes Spotify's model is the concept of 'loosely coupled, tightly aligned squads.' The key belief here is that 'alignment enables autonomy—the greater the alignment, the more autonomy you can grant.'" A leader's job is to identify the problem and communicate it. The teams can then collaborate to find the best solution.

And what about time constraints? It's true, managers are often overworked and spend so much time in so many meetings that they often have to spend evenings catching up on email and staying up-to-date with what their own boss wants, much less what their employees need. But if you think about it in terms of priorities and the big picture, it's important to ask yourself whether spending extra time guiding your employees, providing context, and helping steer their priorities is worth it. Delegation is fine in theory, but in practice it requires managers to make the extra effort to ensure the delegated tasks are prioritized and done well.

In the end, I would argue there's actually no question at all. If you ensure your employees succeed in the areas you want them to do well in, then haven't you succeeded as well? And one tactic to instituting big picture as well as day-to-day focus within your team is pairing your novice employees with the more expert ones, as we'll discuss in more detail in the next section.

Apprenticeship

The proliferation of management practices in the 1970s and 1980s by prominent business schools across the country has undoubtedly made managers more efficient and productive. Indeed, together with technology gains, the productivity of the average worker shot up 74 percent between 1973 and 2013, according to the Economic Policy Institute (Mishel, Gould, and Bivens 2015). However, I think it's fair to wonder whether a side effect of those practices has been to turn accountability into another word for productivity (which it isn't), touting results over process.

While the productivity boon was great news for corporations, stocks, and shareholders, it has proved a more complex reality for managers. For one, they are working harder and longer than ever before. According to the latest data available from sources such as Gallup, the average full-time employee now works 47 hours per week, up from 40.3 hours in 1970—that's almost a full day more (Saad 2014; Whaples 2001).

However, this increased work time hasn't always translated into more time spent with employees. Alan Patterson, a noted management guru and consultant, said, "It used to be managers could take employees under their wing and develop them steadily, almost like an apprenticeship, giving them feedback, teaching them the ropes." Today, however, management often amounts to little more than a shortcut, he continues, with pressed-for-time managers simply giving employees task-based and deadline-focused direction—little that inspires, involves, or makes employees feel accountable for results in the greater picture.

This is where an apprenticeship approach can make a difference. One of the things I loved about *U.S. News & World Report* was the fact that our department had experts in several areas, particularly foreign affairs. Two of the fact-checkers who worked at the magazine were retired State Department foreign service officers, Erick and Dan. Having traveled and lived all over the world, they were invaluable to the department and proved to be a wellspring of knowledge about many countries and regions. Erick and Dan would regale us with stories about the places they'd been. In doing so, we not only heard fascinating stories, but also learned the basics of our craft—what sources to use to check certain facts, how to call sources on the phone, and, most important, when to question the facts in an article based on our own experience and knowledge.

When I was just starting at the magazine, Kathleen had me work with Erick and Dan, almost in an apprenticeship-type role. I remember once that Dan was fact-checking a story on Turkey and one of our top writers had named a certain market in Istanbul, describing it in vivid detail. Dan, who had lived in Istanbul, sent an email to the writer saying that the market she described wasn't the one she named, but the Grand Bazaar, which, to this day, remains one of the city's finest merchant centers. The writer replied that indeed, she had confused the two markets in her sourcing and was grateful to Dan for catching her mistake.

What was remarkable about that exchange wasn't that he caught the mistake without being on-site with her as she was writing the report—it was that I learned that I could challenge a top writer on something they reported on as being true. That may not seem like a big deal to someone on the outside, but many of these writers at *U.S. News* were national figures at the top of their craft, and a fact-checker wouldn't generally challenge the validity of their reporting. What I learned from watching Dan, however, was that challenging writers was part of the job—and it was done in the name of making the magazine more reputable.

That's where the lost art of apprenticeship comes in. When you as an employee can watch someone with more tenure than you do something—handle a situation, carry themselves, or even simply organize something—the experience can be invaluable. An apprenticeship helps employees learn their craft in a way that can't be replicated.

To me, it's the primary difference between being productive and being accountable. Accountability is not just finishing a task on time; it means taking true responsibility and buying in to the importance of the work's quality. It also takes a much longer-term view because it's not just about the fact that the work is done, but it's that the work is done well and employees continue to be motivated. Accountability breeds sustainability. That's why apprenticeships, whether formal or informal, can be so effective in helping employees build sustainable habits.

Yet despite evidence that apprenticeships improve productivity and accountability, they are rarely used in the United States. In fact, among developed nations, France, Germany, and the United Kingdom all outstrip the United States in terms of formal apprenticeships on an absolute basis, according to the Center for American Progress (Steinberg and Gurwitz 2014).

And that's just formal apprenticeships. In the average workplace, informal apprenticeships have all but disappeared. It's not surprising because managers lack the time to facilitate an apprenticeship-like atmosphere or pair employees with those they can learn from on the job. When pressed for time, what does the average person do? Well, first, they take shortcuts. For a manager, that often means they delegate tasks they don't want to handle and turn the management process into a list of things for employees to do. It's not that they don't want to do more, but that's all they have the time to communicate.

How do you get around this when you're likely in the same situation? Won't most people simply continue to get busier and have less time?

Part of your journey to being a good manager or executive is understanding the difference between short-term productivity and long-term employee growth. As a manager, giving employees a list of tasks and demanding they get them done may improve short-term productivity, but over the long term, it's not clear that this is effective in helping people get better at what they do or stay motivated. Your focus must be on both.

If you don't have time to personally look at how employees learn how to do their jobs well, then you are probably negatively influencing the long-term viability of those employees. Developing accountability in your staff also means that you make time for them. This involves finding ways to motivate, inspire, and challenge them.

Challenge

What does it mean to challenge your employees? Every manager will define this differently, but I would separate this phrase into a few different areas, again with a focus on caring about employee development. In particular, managers should make sure any challenges are achievable, long term, and meaningful.

Achievable

Let's start with an achievable challenge. Outside of simply not asking anything from employees, I think one of the biggest mistakes that managers make is that they don't understand when or how much to push an employee's capacity to work. For example, if you think that a poorly performing employee who gives a "2" for effort will somehow turn into a "10" just because you challenge them, you're probably going to be let down. Rather, you need to focus on building capacity in employees over time. And that takes understanding a little bit about the brain and what constitutes an achievable challenge.

To illustrate this, think about a video game, such as Nintendo's Super Mario Galaxy series. When you load any well-designed game, it starts at a very easy level. It's designed so that anyone who is new to the experience can learn as they go and gradually get better, while those who are already skilled can breeze through. Each level gets slightly harder than the last—the enemies move quicker, the controls require more dexterity—but the game builds on the skills the player has already acquired. As a result, each level poses a greater challenge. It's the reason games are so addictive—even though a player might not complete a particular level, they can see what it takes to reach the goal and become more motivated to get there. If a game started at a level that was too difficult, or neglected to build up a player's skills effectively, most people would simply give up.

Management follows a similar principle. Your goal is to help your employees become continuously better at what they do. Hence, you have to give them challenges that are achievable so they can build their capacity at their current level. Challenges that are too hard—or too different from the work they do now—will likely overwhelm them, and many workers will simply get frustrated or give up.

How do you determine the appropriate challenge? Part of that comes from understanding the work employees do and how long a task takes. If you don't understand that, it's hard to communicate appropriate deadlines, and it becomes even more difficult to create an appropriate challenge. Good managers find out how long a task may take or try it themselves so they can understand the challenges involved. Only at that point can you set dates on deliverables with any reasonable sense of achievability.

And the key phrase here is *setting the dates.* Many managers communicate tasks and deliverables (and even priorities), but they never set an actual date that creates a sense of urgency to get tasks done. The result is that the average employee has neither the goal nor the drive to finish something in a particular timeframe. The bottom line: If you set dates and follow up, your teams will be more accountable for getting things done with a sense of urgency.

Long Term Versus Short Term

Next, let's discuss long-term challenges. After more than 25 years in business, I believe the biggest mistake companies make is neglecting long-term thinking and development in favor of a short-term, quarterly (or annual) results mentality. For example, companies are often slow to move resources from old product lines that still earn revenue to potential new revenue lines because their priorities remain focused on the current year. Business writer and management consultant Peter Drucker (2009) once called this behavior "slaughtering tomorrow's opportunity on the altar of yesterday."

Drucker's admonishment, though, isn't just about broader company practices. It applies to management as well. How many managers do you know who focus on their team's immediate needs based on the quarterly or annual results? Probably a lot, right? "We have to hit our numbers" is the rallying cry of so many divisions across so many companies. But part of accountability is also ensuring the financial security of the organization not just this year but next year and the year after as well.

The challenge for you as a manager and one that you must pass along to your employees is how to hit this quarter's numbers while also developing the tools, platforms, products, delivery systems, marketing capabilities, and so forth that you need for the future. That's actually the hardest part about being accountable—putting structures in place to grow the business for the long term.

One thing you can do that I find particularly helpful is to develop pipeline-like structures you can use for product, marketing, or any other type of longer-term initiative. What is it you want to produce next year? The year after? Based on what resources? Think this through and then map out the foundations for deliverables that will allow your team to hit the dates you set. Meet regularly to check on the progress.

For example, for longer-term initiatives, I meet with my team monthly, and in some case biweekly, to discuss development. That helps ensure longer-term initiatives remain top of mind for staff, so they understand that tomorrow's initiatives can't be ignored.

Meaningful

Finally, let's talk about making challenges meaningful. And maybe the best way to illustrate this is with another example from my *U.S. News & World Report* days.

After leaving the fact-checking department and becoming a reporter, I remember once working with the managing editor of the business section on a story that I pitched and was approved to go forward. I wrote the first draft of the story, which was about the decline of the horse-racing industry, and sent it to the editor. It was a topic he knew a little bit about.

After reading my article, he said one thing to me: "You know how many times you're going to write this story before we get it right?"

"How many times?" I asked.

"Four times—until we get it right," was his reply.

"Couldn't I get it right on the next try?" I thought to myself, but given that I was simply a junior reporter, I didn't say anything. After all, he was an experienced editor who had worked at the *New York Times* and *Wall Street Journal*. I walked out of his office saying to myself that this was going to be painful.

And I was right.

Do you know how many times I rewrote that piece? I rewrote it exactly four times. And when he did his final edit on the last version, it was probably one he had planned out from my first version of the story. Over the course of those edits, I added some additional details, but the essential story basically remained the same.

So, what was the point of writing that piece three additional times? The editor wanted to show me that he was in charge. Was it challenging? It certainly was. But the larger point is that the information he made me fix and the extra work he made me do had no effect on the end product, aside from conveying the lesson he wanted to teach me. To this day, I remember this experience as an example of behavior that serves no purpose other than to reinforce the idea that as a manager, you have a certain control over an employee. And in the end, he lost many writers due to this behavior.

The point is, managers must make the challenges meaningful—both as they relate to the overall unit goals and the company at large. If you challenge employees to perform a task without any meaningful goal in mind, you'll end up wasting both your time and the employee's time. In many cases, you also risk creating a dispiriting environment where employees begin to think they are being picked on for no reason. That's why the challenge should be put into the context of moving the needle for the company. This not only helps motivate employees, but pushes the intrinsic accountability they feel in their jobs.

So, what's the trick to understanding whether challenges are meaningful? Ask yourself: Does the task align with the overall goals of the unit or the company? Does it help them get better at something? Finally, does the challenge have an impact on the end product? If you can't answer yes to any of those questions, you might have to ask what your true motivation is.

In the end, managers should challenge their employees with development opportunities that are achievable, long-term oriented, and meaningful. To gain buy-in, managers must also embed a culture of lifelong learning in their teams.

Education

One of the wonderful things about having a boss that loves learning things is that they will often establish an environment where education becomes infectious. Isn't that the type of environment any manager would want to create? An atmosphere where employees learn new things while they're on the job.

As fact-checkers at *U.S. News & World Report,* we had a unique situation in that our job required us to learn new things every day by reading and fact-checking stories about different parts of the world, new cultures, or new scientific discoveries. It made for an environment where just doing your job meant you were getting the equivalent of an additional bachelor's degree in world affairs.

But our boss, Kathleen, also possessed a unique mindset about the job. She was excited to learn anything new—and I mean anything. If one of us told stories about a part of the world we had been to, she sometimes took notes. If she didn't know the answer to a question, even one that wasn't work related, she would go up to the *U.S. News* library (which was several floors above ours) to find the answer, and then she'd come back and report her findings. Remember, this was before the days of Google and endless information at our fingertips.

I like to say she was, in her own way, my first model of the importance of instilling an educational focus in employees. Following her lead, many of us would also look up anything we didn't know. Curiosity about one thing led to curiosity about something else, and each new piece of knowledge made us want to learn something else and share it with the group. In short, we broadened our knowledge and became better fact-checkers thanks to the intellectual environment Kathleen created.

This is the golden opportunity I've seen so many managers miss. They think management is simply about getting things done. And that's certainly part of it. But managers can get too myopic—looking at their employees as means to an end or more like a machine that completes tasks—and fail to recognize that their employees possess a desire to learn, improve, and get better at what they do. They don't instill curiosity or the importance of education because they're looking at only whether the employee finishes, not whether they learn anything, despite the latter being a truer measure of increased employee performance and accountability over time.

This often comes up when there's a critical need for a creative solution. I pity managers who suddenly tell their team, "OK, we need to innovate on this one," without understanding that they must first create an environment that promotes innovative thinking.

Innovation is not an event. After all, how creative will your employees be if all you've ever done is assign them rote tasks to complete? Creativity and innovation come about because your employees can apply knowledge from several different disciplines to a work-related issue. This means that education and continuous learning are critical for creating and solving the hard issues companies often face. For example, consider Apple co-founder Steve Jobs. Through various positions at Hewlett-Packard and Atari, Jobs certainly had the grounding in technology and indeed helped Steve Wozniak build the first Apple I computer. But when asked about the secret of Apple's success years later, he credited his liberal arts background—beauty, form, style—for making the Mac, iPod, iPhone, and iPad the elegant, high-end products they turned out to be.

At the iPad 2 unveiling, Jobs said: "It is in Apple's DNA that technology alone is not enough—it's technology married with liberal arts, married with the humanities, that yields us the results that make our heart sing" (Lehrer 2011).

While Steve Jobs is perhaps an extreme example of innovation, the point should not be lost on you as a manager that the educational atmosphere that you create within your business unit, division, or company can have a significant impact on your team's ability to innovate when the time comes.

Think about it—the more your employees know about the world, people, the arts, science, technology, and business, the more they will be able to creatively apply that diverse knowledge to solve the problems you need as a team. And while innovation doesn't seem like it relates to accountability on the surface, it can be a huge aspect of how teams perform over time because part of accountability is continuing to change and evolve. After all, teams that don't innovate rarely last long in today's competitive era. And if managers don't think long term and neglect to create an atmosphere where education and innovation thrive, are they really being accountable over the long term?

So, how do you create an educational-focused atmosphere as a manager? One thing you can do is continuously provide a different frame of reference from what your employees are used to. For example, people around the office often make fun of me for sliding in references to things from the 1970s or 1980s, long before many of my staff had been born. The reaction I get is often: *Why do you do that? It's not like they're going to know what you're talking about!*

Perhaps (admittedly) I do that intentionally to seem "old," but it's also a way to give my staff a window into how to connect with people like me, who may not share their generational view. I also hope to pique their interest in other decades—whether it's the arts, music, movies, sports—to give them something that someone else my generation or older might connect to.

The point is, learning doesn't have to be strictly tied to those areas that directly affect job performance. And it doesn't have to happen in a classroom—learning can be fun, casual, and lighthearted! People can learn about anything, anywhere, but it's up to you to create an atmosphere that introduces people to new ideas or concepts both inside and outside their areas of responsibility.

It works because accountability, to a great extent, involves connection with audiences, other divisions, and, most of all, bosses. Your staff may not be able to do their jobs well unless they can connect on a human level. So, the more you as a manager can foster an environment where your staff can learn, the better chance they'll have to connect with someone else. And the better their connections, the more potential they'll have to translate that into greater accountability in the long run.

Safety

It seems obvious that managers should try to create a safe environment so employees can execute their jobs without fear. But the number of workplaces that are still considered abusive is shocking. Think of the countless brand-name organizations caught up in the #MeToo movement that have now been exposed as failing to trust and protect their female employees. In fact, according to some studies, 75 percent of employees in the United States are or have recently been subject to workplace bullying, defined as "repeated, health-harming mistreatment of one or more persons (the targets) by one or more perpetrators" by the Workplace Bullying Institute (Comaford 2016).

Consider, for example, the revelations of alleged harassment at Sterling Jewelers, the multibillion-dollar company behind the Jared the Galleria of Jewelry and Kay Jewelers retail brands. According to sworn statements filed by 250 women and men who worked at Sterling, female employees at the company throughout the late 1990s and 2000s "were routinely groped, demeaned and urged to sexually cater to their bosses to stay employed" (Harwell 2017). These allegations were outlined in a 2017 report by the *Washington Post*. A Sterling spokesman denied the accusations, saying in the same *Post* report that they had "thoroughly investigated the allegations and have concluded they are not substantiated by the facts and certainly do not reflect our culture."

While the purpose of this chapter isn't to discuss the merits of the case either way, note what Ellen Contaldi, a Sterling manager between 1994 and 2008 and one of the 250 employees, said in an interview that was later released by the *Post*. "I didn't like being alone, anywhere. I used to dread going [to the meetings]," she said. "If you were even remotely attractive or outgoing, which most salespeople are, you were meat, being shopped."

It probably goes without saying that any manager or managers who create such a hostile environment likely impede the desire of employees to want to work at that company, much less feel any sense of accountability. And certainly, the allegations in the Sterling case are the more extreme end of the spectrum.

Hostile managers are also known to take credit for their employees' good work, while throwing them under the bus if an outcome is undesirable. In effect, this practice turns out looking more like conditional accountability. This behavior may be linked to narcissism. For narcissists, according to psychologist Susan Krauss Whitbourne (2012), self-esteem can become dependent on "having that position in the spotlight." So when a project succeeds, narcissistic managers will seek adoration and praise from others. But if the project fails, they'll likely try to distance themselves by placing the blame on others to protect their fragile sense of self.

"Their emotional lives become dominated by the need to be recognized and they go increasingly out of their way to ensure this need is satisfied," Whitbourne continues. "They insist on receiving special treatment, complain when they don't get it, and reject people who they feel get in their way." Of course, no one really wants to take responsibility for a failure, but it should be owned by the person or team responsible, as should any successful project. When a direct report is successful and thriving, that naturally reflects on their manager; there's no need to take credit or boast about the success, others will recognize it.

Yet, hostile work environments fostered by bad bosses continue to persist at workplaces across the country. Why? I think that it in part comes from the mistaken belief that managers can inspire accountability by intimidating and instilling fear in their employees. But while that may seem effective on the surface, it's rarely sustainable over time. And when factoring in health costs related to stress, missed work, lost productivity, and other issues most companies pay for, bad managers may actually be costing the company more than they're gaining by intimidating employees.

That's why safety—creating a productive environment where employees don't feel threatened—is a top priority for managers.

What constitutes a safe environment? Well, I'm going to skip over the obvious—that employees need to have a workplace free from fear and intimidation, whether that's bullying, harassment, or even threats of physical violence. It should go without saying that if you foster an environment like that, you have worse things to worry about (such as lawsuits) than employee accountability.

Instead, I want to focus on three areas that may not seem obvious, but can have a big impact on employees doing their work and doing it well: early communication, positivity, and risk taking.

Early Communication

Other chapters in this book will focus on the importance of good communication as part of the overall ACCEL model. And good communication by managers certainly has a big impact on overall team accountability. However, for the purposes of this section, I'd like to discuss a more narrow aspect of communication as it relates to creating a safe environment—in particular, the art of telegraphing information to employees.

Let me start with a story. When my kids were younger, I remember my wife and I would often be rushing around going from one thing to the next, which sometimes meant veering from an established routine. If you have young kids, you know that the minute you veer from the established routine your kids become extremely upset, particularly if you mention something at the last minute.

In my desire to avoid these outbursts, I began to telegraph the activities our family would do further in advance. So, if we were choosing a restaurant, for example, instead of doing it randomly at the last minute we would create a schedule that said one person could choose a restaurant we'd go to that week and then rotate it. That longer-term planning helped the child who didn't get to choose accept the idea of going to his sibling's choice instead. And for me, it meant escaping another meltdown.

Adults are also creatures of habit, and they don't like change either. So, if you're going to change up an established routine, it's important to telegraph those changes as far in advance as you can, otherwise it may come across as a threat. As a manager, you need to communicate information in advance so employees can prepare themselves for the change.

To give you an example, my employer, the Association for Talent Development, underwent a website redesign in 2017, which would involve my team's participation. In conjunction with the redesign we had developed a new topical taxonomy for our content that had to be assigned to older, archived content before the transfer could happen. As you can imagine, implementing a new taxonomy isn't easy, and my team would have to prioritize this work in addition to their daily duties.

One of the things I tried to do was telegraph this work far in advance. So I let my team know this was coming a couple months before the "tagging" period started. While they weren't all that happy about the project, having that information up front helped them process it. It also allowed them to adjust their schedules to have enough time to take on this extra task.

But imagine if I had sprung this task on them the day before: "Surprise! You'll be doing additional work, and you'll have only a limited time to complete it." Almost certainly there would have been an uproar—and rightly so. As an employee, I would've felt taken advantage of if a boss did that to me.

Yet, I've seen so many managers who don't communicate larger initiatives early. They wait, then they forget, and then a day or two before something starts, they spring the task on the employee. What happens in those cases is that the employee suddenly feels unsettled (unsafe) in that environment because it's no longer predictable.

Understandably, there are certainly times when there's no getting around that. But if you constantly create unsettling environments because you don't telegraph messages, you are inviting unnecessary drama and uncertainty where there doesn't need to be. And, as far as accountability goes, such environments can easily distract focus from the key tasks you need employees to complete.

Risk

One of my favorite quotes of the modern business era comes from Mark Zuckerberg, the founder of Facebook. "The biggest risk is not taking any risk. In a world that's changing really quickly, the only strategy that is guaranteed to fail is not taking risks," he told an audience at Y Combinator's Startup School event in 2011 (Tobak 2011).

What Zuckerberg understands, as other leaders do, is that risk is a necessary element of today's business environment. To move ahead, companies need to try new things, enter new markets, and look beyond current product lines.

Yet modern management is rife with examples of companies and managers trying to lead as risk-free of an existence as they can. They keep employees focused on short-term tasks that they know "get the job done," and they hesitate to try something that hasn't been done before. They don't want to stick their (or their team's) necks out any farther by working on something new in case something goes wrong.

It's a mindset that not only is debilitating for employees, but hampers their ability to learn and become accountable over the long term. Managers need to create an atmosphere where employees are empowered to take risks. Of course, to a certain extent, risk taking is part of a broader company culture that managers can't control, but they can—and should—take actions to foster risk taking.

Why?

Risk is an essential part of development, not only as a company, but for individuals. Managers need to create a safe environment where failure is not only tolerated but encouraged as a way to learn something new. Consider this quote from Richard Branson (2014), the founder of British multinational conglomerate Virgin Group:

> *Curiosity is one of humanity's most healthy instincts. Without it we would never have evolved, advanced, or achieved anything. Entrepreneurs who are curious, who listen to what the world is saying, and who learn from hardships and mistakes, will almost certainly be more successful than those who aren't, don't or won't. Remember, if you fall flat on your face, at least you are moving forward!*

It's a great sentiment for sure. But how do you create an environment in which it's safe to take risks? I think part of the answer comes from building risk into future plans and challenging employees to focus on executing for this year as well as the year after. In other words, make risk the norm—make it part of the daily mindset to try new things that could solve core issues that your unit, division, or company is facing. But remember that there is a limit to good failure. I would draw the line at failing at the same thing over and over again. What you want, as a manager, is for the employee to learn from past failures and keep getting better at what they do.

Something I like to do is reconsider our strategies and operations a few times a year so we can make adjustments and outline tactics for new areas or plans we have beyond the next 12 months. I begin by asking: What should we do next year? What's our opportunity? What does the market look like? Then I put a structure in place so employees can tackle the steps in a reasonable timeframe to not only begin answering the questions but also execute on new opportunities.

Sometimes we've succeeded and sometimes we've failed. But even when we fail it's OK because we learned something in the process and made adjustments the next time we tried a similar approach.

Positivity

Similar to creating a safe environment for risk by embracing the possibility of failure is for managers to encourage positivity. And by this, I don't mean playing Pollyanna or denying reality if things are difficult or challenging. It's fine to acknowledge that life can be tough. What I mean by encouraging positivity is fostering an atmosphere that discourages excessive negativity or complaining. I believe that as a manager, you're a model for how employees believe they also should behave. So, if you complain about things, they most certainly will too.

I remember once working with a very talented co-worker who was really good at his job and managed a large team at a company I had worked for. But every day, he would complain about his boss or the direction of the company or how stupid everything was. Soon, it became hard to be around that person; even if you wanted to take a positive attitude about work, you couldn't because this individual brought everybody down.

Was the general work environment to blame for this? It probably didn't help, because the person wasn't wrong in many of his observations. But the larger point as you think about accountability is that this individual didn't add anything to the solution—his complaining only encouraged others to do the same, which created a very demotivating environment.

I think this is where mindset plays a big role as a manager. Even in challenging situations, the onus is on you to ensure your team takes a positive, solutions-oriented approach. When you complain, you are signaling that the world revolves around what you do—that you believe you are entitled to something you didn't get. And you are saying it's OK for your employees to be similarly self-absorbed.

It's a bad message all around.

I remember Kathleen used to say to me: "I'm fine if you tell me a problem. But you also have to come to me with a solution if you want me to help." It's a lesson I never forgot. The climate you create has to be positive in the sense that it's solutions focused. Bad things are going to happen. But what separates a good manager from a bad one is how they deal with the situation and the attitude they take toward it.

In the end, positivity breeds positivity. And negativity breeds negativity. Think about how your message comes across. "Work sucks and I hate it" is one approach. Alternatively, think how powerful it could be if your underlying message is, "We can do this. Together. Regardless of how challenging the problem." I think you and your employees will be happier (and feel more accountable) if you choose the latter.

Performance Management

Finally, let's touch on the topic of performance management. At many companies, the process hasn't changed that much: Near the beginning of the year, employees enter their goals, which are ideally aligned with the company's broader business objectives, as well as measurable and achievable. They also may list areas to improve and suggestions for learning activities they can complete during the year. Managers then sign off on the goals and send them to the HR department, which typically runs the process.

Then, in many places, those data go into a black hole—neither the manager nor the employee looks at the goals or talks about them until the annual review. If things change during the year—such as readjusting goals or benchmarks—the manager simply takes that into account during the review period. Aside from the documentation issues needed from a dispute-resolution standpoint, managers rarely feel the need to dig into the data all that much. Indeed, the typical manager enjoys the performance management process about as much as they do a hangover—it's tolerated because it's the price of focusing on what they'd rather be doing.

There's quite a bit of discussion about moving from an annual review process to more of an ongoing conversation, which is something that many best-practice organizations are doing. While these organizational decisions often lie within HR and seem beyond the scope of the average manager, the implications regarding accountability are clear: As a manager, you should meet regularly with your staff to go over where they are, how they're tracking toward goals, what challenges they're facing, and what feedback you can give to help them improve.

If you adopt the FACES model, you will naturally take these steps because the framework is built with an eye toward more contact with your direct reports and your staff within the larger division. And regardless of whether you schedule a "review" on an annual or more frequent basis, if you've been doing your job as a manager by giving more frequent feedback and providing more focused direction, nothing in your review process should come as a surprise. Even if you still don't like to do performance reviews, as "hangovers" go, the headache will most certainly be mild compared with how you might typically approach it today.

Conclusion

One of the most interesting discussions you can watch on YouTube involves the topic of accountability and the great chef Thomas Keller, founder of the Michelin 3-star restaurant French Laundry—in Yountville, California—and the sister establishment Per Se in New York. Interviewed at Stanford's Graduate School of Business in 2013, Keller talked about the importance of developing chefs to be better than he was. He said, "I run a sports franchise the way I describe it. . . . We have to be thinking generationally about who is coming up. Who is going to be replacing whom? And how we're going to do that. How we're hiring, how we're mentoring, how we're training our staff so that they can become—sooner or later—the franchise player" (Keller 2013).

It's a fascinating mindset in that it focuses on training staff to eventually leave and start their own business (which is what many of the chefs under Keller have done). Yet, what comes through most of all when you watch the video is Keller's dedication to the development of his chefs in such a high-pressure environment. Indeed, underlying his philosophy is this focus on a kind of mutual accountability—that Keller and his top chefs invest the time with more inexperienced chefs they hire to continuously train them and provide feedback and, in turn, collaborate to generate new ideas. That, to Keller, is what it means to care about the people under him—to make them better and better at what they do every day and become accountable for the highest-quality results.

Being a good manager is hard. And of all parts of the ACCEL framework, ensuring your team's accountability may rank as the most difficult to achieve, simply because it requires the most energy on the part of a manager. After all, managers should not only be mutually vested in accountability with their employees, but they must also take the time to create all the foundations of accountability to be truly successful.

So why the FACES model?

I think what's difficult about managing is that it often seems like we, as managers, ask employees to do tasks and finish work that is hard or difficult, and while doing so we may feel bad for even asking. In that environment, our mindset becomes one of managing tasks rather than managing people, and we lose sight of what motivates or inspires intrinsic accountability.

Underlying the FACES approach is the idea that managers want to help employees get better. That they will invest the time to make it so. That managers communicate the fact that they care about the long-term development and improvement of their staff. That they model behavior and assign tasks that will help their employees have an impact on the unit and the company as a whole.

In other words, employees need to believe that their managers have their long-term interests at heart. If you follow the FACES model and invest the time, I think it's a good bet that employees will give you their full support and become more accountable, making you and the team look good when it comes to the end results. And for a little extra investment on your part, that would seem to be a big payoff.

2

Communication

Ken O'Quinn

Dave Samson once had to fly from San Francisco to Texas to tell an employee his job was in jeopardy. He told the person, "When you leave here we will have a plan [for improvement]."

"It was a partnership. We were in it together to deal with the situation," Samson recalled. "My approach is, I understand this person is struggling, but I want them to be successful."

Communication skill is essential to managing, because the ability to write, speak, and listen is directly tied to attaining your and your organization's goals. Managers and leaders guide, direct, and motivate others, and they are judged by how well their teams and organizations achieve results. Without communication, there can be no motivation, no leadership, no productivity, and no organization (Goldhaber et al. 1984).

The strong link between good communication practices and improved performance might be reflected in the sheer amount of time that many managers and executives in the 21st century spend in informational interactions—much more than their predecessors. For example, a Swedish study found that CEOs spend at least 69 percent of their time providing information, listening to it, or discussing it. That's because they operate in a more decentralized manner than previous leaders. They delegate more authority to managers, so they need to devote more energy to communicating their expectations, vision, strategy, and performance targets (Tengblad 2006). In turn, managers also delegate work to their own direct reports, creating a cascading effect of information flow.

Managers Need to Appreciate Language

Total Quality Management (TQM), Six Sigma, One Minute Management, and Excellence are but a few of the trendy management systems that have consumed the attention of managers and their organizations in recent decades. These models, as well as such words as *empowerment, engagement,* and *performance improvement,* all involve communication. But what gets lost in the preoccupation with buzzwords is that managing is about action, and language is at the heart of motivating employees to get things done.

"Managers have to learn to know language, to understand what words are and what they mean," wrote management guru Peter Drucker (1954). "Without ability to motivate by means of the written and spoken word or the telling number, a manager cannot be successful."

Many businesspeople scoff at rhetoric as a management tool, dismissing it as the empty hype and bluster of political speeches, or something high school students learn on the debate team. However, rhetoric is rooted in the works of Greek philosophers, who taught us how to use language to argue persuasively. Managers—and the people they manage—will always benefit from honing their rhetoric and language skills.

Rhetoric is about word choice and the skillful use of language, which can be useful to managers in every communication, including email, policy statements, short reports, town hall meetings, and formal speeches. Language, whether in a verbal or nonverbal communication form, is certainly important to the aspects of a manager's job that we will discuss in this chapter:

- **Being transparent.** The words you use can determine your credibility, which is essential to motivating people—choose wisely.

- **Influencing your team.** By becoming more transparent and credible, you can tailor your message to different direct reports, with the hope of influencing them to act, whether it's to complete a task or assume a developmental opportunity.
- **Delivering actionable feedback.** When the situation is uncomfortable, delivering criticism clearly and constructively can ease the tension. You need to be candid, but you can be respectfully direct and use a neutral tone to have a productive exchange.
- **Running effective team meetings.** As a manager, you will often need to schedule and lead meetings with your direct reports, and sometimes you'll need to communicate group feedback. Meetings with your direct reports, whether face-to-face or virtual, are opportunities to draw on everyone's expertise and solve problems. Preparation is essential for respecting everyone's time and delivering on meeting goals. Provide a detailed agenda, make people feel comfortable enough to contribute, and be sure people leave knowing their assignments and deadlines.

An Overview of Developments in Management Communication

1936
Dale Carnegie's book *How to Win Friends and Influence People* introduced the idea that interpersonal skills, not rank or salary, are what build and strengthen a person's credibility.

1950s
Behavioral research began to focus on a manager's behavior, including communication. Economics, anthropology, psychology, and sociology are all applied to understanding communication on the job.

1960

David Berlo, building on an earlier concept, introduced the sender-message-channel-receiver (SMCR) communication model, which highlighted where communications can break down.

1978

A group of management communication professors from elite MBA programs met at Yale to discuss their programs, which were in their infancy. The group formed the Managerial Communicators Association (MCA), which continues to meet annually.

1980s

U.S. companies maintained a hierarchical management system, with managers issuing directives and employees following instructions. At quarterly meetings, executives would take questions but avoided elaborate answers and steered clear of discussing bad news. When Douglas Fraser, president of the United Automobile Workers Union, was given a seat on the Chrysler Board of Directors, he encouraged sharing of information in the face of foreign competition. His effort helped legitimize more openness.

1998

Amid the dot-com boom, technology created new ways to get work done, and knowledge became more important than merely taking directions and performing rote tasks. The complexity of technology required that people ask questions and converse with others to reach common understanding. Management needed to communicate.

2000s

The Internet and social media provided universal access to information. For the first time, customers and employees could vocalize their complaints and opinions, which pressured companies to be more responsive and more candid.

2001-2002

Financial scandals at Enron, WorldCom, Tyco, and others led to the demand for more transparent communication.

2002-Present
Scandals and the responses of management continued to taint public perceptions of corporate executives.

2013
The reputation of British Petroleum (BP) plunged after the Deepwater Horizon oil rig explosion. The company was slow to take responsibility and blamed others for the disaster, which killed 11 workers.

2015
The EPA found that Volkswagen had cheated on emissions tests by installing devices that allowed the cars to exceed pollution limits when they were not being tested. An auto-industry survey found that public perception of VW car quality had dropped 27 percent.

◇◇

Being Transparent

Dictionaries define *transparent* as "so fine in texture that you can see through it" or "easily understood, very clear, open, frank, candid." Conversationally, we would describe transparency as, "She's the real deal" or "What you see is what you get."

In the workplace, transparency is an openness and sincerity that creates the perception that a leader is credible. Jerome Sullivan (2018), who developed Motivational Language Theory, says behaving in a transparent manner is essential to inspiring others: "Transparent managers are open about their own needs and interests, their values, and desires. This kind of openness is authentic, in that the manager is not lying to himself or others." The implication here is that a manager who is not honest and trustworthy will not attract followers.

Although management experts and scholars have written and spoken for decades about the importance of strong communication between management and employees, the need for transparency in management did not become a significant issue until the late 1980s and early 1990s.

In a traditional, hierarchical corporate structure, managers weren't encouraged to be transparent and weren't taught to be motivational or emotionally expressive. But in the last 40 years, as employees became increasingly aware of inconsistencies between what management said and what it did, they started expecting "managers to 'walk the walk,' not just make high-minded speeches and go back to the old ways of doing things," says Alan Csiky (2018), a communications manager at General Motors. "Alignment became important."

As more companies recognized that top-down communication had limited success, two-way communication became the practice, with management soliciting feedback and encouraging employees to ask questions.

John Case coined the term *open-book management* in an *Inc.* magazine article in 1990, amid a financial crisis, when he called on companies to be more forthcoming with information and to help employees understand it. He emphasized the word *management:* "There's no point in opening the books unless employees are empowered to use the information to make good decisions—to move the numbers in the right direction" (Case 2018).

After the collapse of Enron, WorldCom, and Arthur Andersen shook financial markets in 2001 and 2002, employees and shareholders began demanding full disclosure, not only about financial information for shareholders but also about the reasons behind management decisions in the daily operation of the business. Investors, voters, and employees wanted accountability.

Here are several ways managers, and leaders, can be transparent through their use of language.

Match Words With Actions

As a manager, when you act in ways that are consistent with what you advocate in written messages and spoken presentations, you strengthen your credibility. When you "walk the walk," people see that you live by your word, and trust develops. The more trust you foster, the more transparent both parties are.

"Communication comes in both words and deeds, and the latter are often the most powerful form," said John Kotter (1995), a leadership expert and Harvard Business School professor. "Nothing undermines change more than behavior by important individuals that is inconsistent with their words."

When actions are consistent with words, managers demonstrate behavioral integrity, which is essential to building credibility in the eyes of employees. If you say you'll make decisions collaboratively, such as project planning decisions, do not go into your office, write the project plan by yourself, and then ask everyone to sign off on it. That's a broken promise; transparency and trust are lost.

Kent Thiry, CEO of DaVita Medical Group, one of the country's largest kidney care companies, advocates building a community within his workforce. He has even suited up in a three musketeers outfit for employee meetings to reinforce what musketeers stood for: unity of purpose and care for one another.

Building a caring community with a shared sense of purpose means that Thiry expects to be held accountable for his performance. At his interactive employee meetings, Thiry encourages employees to raise their hands and draw his attention to his own shortcomings: "I needed help in my bad habits, and real-time help is better than a 360-degree [performance review]" (Thiry 2018).

He is not alone. Dave Samson, general manager of global public affairs for Chevron, stands in front of his team and tells them what he received for performance feedback and how he plans to improve. One new employee, flabbergasted, told Samson he had never worked for a company where a leader acknowledged qualities he needed to work on.

"How can I expect others to improve?" Samson (2018) asked. "We all have to gain new skills."

Make People Believe You Care About Them

Help your employees grow, get to know them, and recognize their achievements. Even a two-minute chat in the hall can be a meaningful exchange.

"How is your project going?" is a thoughtful inquiry. And people always appreciate it when a manager simply asks, what can I do to help? If something is happening in their personal life and it's appropriate for you to ask, do that.

Frank Blake, former CEO of Home Depot, would spend Sunday afternoons writing more than 100 thank-you notes to store employees for individual accomplishments that had been brought to his attention. He would also host an informal dinner with groups of 10 to 15 employees once a week, whether he was at headquarters in Atlanta or traveling throughout the country. Thinking they would be among a few hundred people at a large event, invited employees were stunned at the intimate setting. "My point was to say everybody in the company is important," explains Blake (2018).

Senior leaders and managers accomplish nothing alone, Blake continues. They depend on others giving their best effort, and "people's interests and enthusiasm about investing in your success hinges on how they see you investing in their success."

Kathryn Yates (2018) had to convey her empathy over a conference call as a global practice leader at a large consulting firm when an economic downturn forced the company to take a drastic step. She had to tell midlevel managers on the call that they needed to trim 10 percent of the workforce, and that all leaders, from senior leadership down to middle management, would have to take a 10 percent pay cut to avoid permanent layoffs. The goal was to return to normal salary levels once the bottom-line rebounded.

"I became emotional," she says, adding that it was hard to ask people to sacrifice that much. But the leaders accepted the cuts and applauded her for being genuine during the phone call. Eventually, the company's performance improved significantly and salaries were able to return to previous levels.

Examples of leaders who retreat to the executive suite and invest little effort in connecting with employees and being authentic are far more abundant. Organizational communications consultant Angela Sinickas worked at a medical-supply company where senior leaders (all researchers) did not want to interact with employees other than in formal meetings and necessary conversations. The leaders even had a special door installed that connected the parking garage to the executive floor of the office building so they could avoid walking through the lobby.

"Some people will never recognize their behavior is wrong," Sinickas (2018) says. "You can't force them to be better at something they can't get good at. You need to work around it."

Demonstrate Behavioral Integrity

The virtues of honesty, authenticity, and ethical behavior can be joined under the broader quality of behavioral integrity, which is essential to transparency.

"People can smell honesty," Thiry says. "People's intuition is incredibly refined. No matter how charismatic you are, people can smell your intentions, your authenticity."

When managers are more authentic, they are more candid about their reasoning behind a decision. The employees not only consider the manager to be honest, but they give more thought to understanding the decision.

"In the old model, power was based on how little I was transparent, so I could 'piece-meal' it," says Chevron's Samson. "Today, power is based on being transparent, because everyone can find out information. You can't hoard it."

Authenticity, often considered synonymous with transparency, is founded on a strong moral compass. An authentic manager takes time to reflect, create a strong sense of self-awareness, and develop a solid ethical code. Communication with others (including direct reports) is genuine and influenced by this code. The result is transparency—honestly sharing all the information that others need.

Being ethical was important to Hodding Carter, the State Department spokesman for President Jimmy Carter. As a member of a well-known Mississippi journalism family, "I came there with a predisposition to openness. It was my starting premise," says Carter (2018). When he knew information but could not disclose it, he told reporters he would reveal as much as he could.

gument for transparency, counterintuitively, is always self-pres-
e explains. "It's not only the right thing to do, it's the smart
uıng to do because it buys something invaluable: It buys you trust." Shareholders, employees, colleagues, and adversaries are more likely to be more
patient in difficult times if you have been forthcoming in the past.

Let People See You Fail

Letting your followers, fellow team members, and other managers and
leaders see that you have failed helps them understand how to react to
and learn from failure. When they fail, they understand that it's not only
acceptable but a positive growth experience within the organization.

When talking with your employees about a project you are about to
embark on, you can tell them, "I know that failure is a possibility, because I
have failed before." But remember to discuss your failures in the context of
how the mistakes led you to where you are today. Similarly, explain to your
team how their disappointing experiences can lead to strong performances.

Influencing Your Team

The traditional hierarchical management model of the 20th century has
passed. Employees are more skeptical today and want to know not only
what they are being asked to do, but why it is necessary and what the
benefit will be. So if managing is about motivating people to get things
done and take action, persuasion is an important skill for managers to have.
Simply being personable, even charismatic, is not enough.

Most people are unfamiliar with the behavioral psychology behind persuasion. This is because the science of influence is rarely taught in high school,
and is only slightly more likely to be found in a college or MBA program. So
when managers sit down to compose a message to persuade someone, they
are not sure where to begin beyond using please and thank you.

Strengthen Your Credibility

The success or failure of a persuasive attempt does not always rest on the
message. The likelihood of success is often determined before you write

the first word. What do people think of you? Aristotle said that to be a persuasive communicator, you can appeal to your audience with a strong argument (logic) or you can reach people emotionally. However, he said that the most important thing was to be viewed as credible, a person of good character.

Credibility is important because people often decide how to respond to your appeal based on what they think of you rather than the content of your message. It is a judgment that the audience makes about your believ-ability (O'Keefe 2002). Social science research shows that people judge credibility primarily by two criteria, expertise and trustworthiness:

- **Expertise.** Be an avid reader of industry magazines, scholarly articles, textbooks, and weekly and daily news sites and publications. Most managers grow to be authorities in their field, in part because they constantly absorb information. You also can strengthen your expertise by making the effort to be part of projects that expand and deepen your knowledge and experience.
- **Trustworthiness.** Be honest and ethical, be a good listener, and don't be afraid to make a decision that will benefit another person, even if it is counter to your best interests.

Analyze the Audience and Context

Many persuasive attempts fail because the persuaders are thinking from their perspective—focusing on what they think is important, what they want to say, and what they think the audience needs to hear. As the communicator, you need to know as much as you can about your audience's thinking so you can shape your message to their beliefs, attitudes, and values as much as possible.

An auto industry executive might want to speak about the virtues of making automotive parts overseas. However, if the audience is the United Automobile Workers union, the speaker might still advocate that position, but will probably want to adjust their presentation.

The way you begin a persuasive message can depend on the audience and the context. Let's look at three scenarios.

Supportive Audience

If you are writing or speaking to people who support the position you are advocating or who generally feel favorably toward you, you can state your point, your recommendation, or your request early in the message and then provide supporting details. There is no need to delay presenting your central idea:

> *Employees have enthusiastically supported our effort to improve efficiency through clear communication, which saves time for the writer and the reader. In keeping with that effort, I am proposing that everyone have a writing buddy, someone who will read your initial drafts of important communication and give you a candid assessment of your writing.*

Resistant Audience

If your audience is skeptical or opposed to your message, you need a different approach. Given the audience's resistance, don't present your main point or position in the opening line or two; instead, start with information the audience already accepts as true. That way, you open on a point of agreement before you begin moving people away from their comfort zone toward a new way of looking at your idea.

If, for example, you want your team to attend a writing workshop, and they do not see the need, here is how you might begin:

> *Nurses, lawyers, and accountants have to be recertified, and we all recognize that this is an important way for them to keep their skills sharp. Yet, when it comes to writing, people assume that what they learned 20 years ago is enough to get them through their careers.*

Complacent Audience

This is a group that is marginally interested, so they need a wake-up call. Jolt your audience with an unusual fact, example, statistic, or anecdote that draws their attention to the importance of the issue and helps create a sense of urgency:

Everyone enjoys the free coffee, snacks, and chilled water available in our company kitchen, but what they don't notice is the trash baskets filled with disposable cups and plates we cannot recycle. It amounts to about 5,000 pounds each year, which is enough to fill a standard swimming pool. Given our commitment to being good corporate citizens of the community, we are asking everyone to bring their own cups to work, along with whatever dishes they need.

Create a Persuasive Message

Once you have the audience's attention, how do you keep them interested so you can influence their thinking?

You probably read or hear several hundred messages a day—advertisements, email requests, fundraising appeals, campaign pitches—all aimed at persuading you to do something. But how many do you remember? A message needs to be compelling to be memorable.

Let's look at some tactics to help make a message more persuasive.

Use Concrete Language

The corporate lexicon is overrun with terms such as *cutting edge, win-win, robust solutions, bulletize, corporate DNA,* and *mission critical,* which clutter communication like an overgrown garden.

These words are stale from excessive use and many are vague—they do not tell readers what you think they do. What does it mean to "up-level" information? Since when is an industry a multifaceted ecosystem?

Most important, in a persuasive context, boring, murky language does not move people. They want to hear the simple, clear language of everyday conversation, the words that great speakers use to make speeches memorable. If John F. Kennedy had said, "Ask not what your country can do for you; ask what you can do to optimize cross-functional leveraging," would people still be talking about that speech today?

Great speakers use concrete language because it relates to real things, real concepts, and real people. The words are familiar and often create imagery. As Brian Fugere and colleagues (2005) at Deloitte and Touche say in *Why Business People Speak Like Idiots,* customers, employees, and shareholders today are crying out for authenticity. They are not inspired by language that sounds artificial or phony.

Get People to Imagine the Outcome

If you are trying to persuade someone to embrace a policy change, explain the positive outcome they can look forward to as a result of the policy. If people visualize something favorable, whether it's the benefits of a new policy or the pleasure of owning a new television, they imagine themselves having that experience. They rehearse it mentally and it becomes an expectation. Because they are confident they can achieve the goal (it is tied to their sense of competence), they are more likely to say yes to a request (Carroll 2010).

This also can be an effective technique if you warn someone about negative consequences. One way to persuade a person not to do something is by suggesting the potential for regret. People are more likely to comply with a request if noncompliance will bring an outcome they wish hadn't happened.

Remember the "Bandwagon" Effect

When you want to persuade someone to do something, let them know how many other people are doing it.

When we are uncertain about what to do in a situation, we often look around to see what others are doing to determine our response. This is referred to in psychology as the principle of social validation. If everyone else is acting a certain way, we view their behavior as a consensus that it must be the correct, practical, or appropriate thing to do—it validates our decision.

That is why advertisements for medical treatments often say something like, "Hundreds of doctors recommend this." Similarly, people use this principle when deciding where to eat: If the parking lot is full or if there are long lines of waiting customers, it must be good food.

So, if you want employees to join the new company fitness center, tell them how many of their co-workers already have. Or if you want someone to attend a meeting or an event, mention who else plans to be there.

Invoke the Consistency Principle

People have a deeply rooted need to be consistent in their behavior, because consistency is a highly regarded character trait. In fact, those who are consistent are viewed as more responsible, reliable, organized, mature, and intellectually superior, while inconsistent people are perceived as inconsiderate, unreliable, and erratic.

People want to be consistent in three ways:

- They want to live up to commitments, because a commitment brings a sense of obligation and they want to follow through on their pledge.
- They want their actions to be consistent with their beliefs, including their beliefs about themselves (their self-image).
- They want to act in ways that are consistent with how they've acted previously.

If you need help on a committee, don't say, "It would be great if you could be part of the group." Instead, present it as a question: "When our committee starts next month, would you be willing to join us?"

If the person says yes, that's a commitment. Then when the committee prepares for its first meeting, go back to the person and remind them: "When we talked last month, you said you would join us on the committee; our first meeting is Tuesday." This increases the likelihood that the person will agree.

When people back out of a commitment, they experience mental turmoil, what psychologists call cognitive dissonance (a theory developed by Leon Festinger in 1957). People like to think of themselves as being responsible, organized, and dependable, so when they are not, their action is inconsistent with their self-image.

Ask for Less Initially

One way to sidestep rejection is to avoid creating resistance at the start (Knowles and Linn 2004). Many persuasive attempts fail because someone makes a large request that is too daunting to the person or the committee that must approve or reject it.

Perhaps you want to add a first-rate training program that has a large price tag, and the decision maker is concerned about other spending needs or other people whose interests will be affected. Rather than asking for the full amount to add the program permanently, you could ask for a lower sum to instead do a pilot program, perhaps for six months. After a successful pilot program, you can ask for the full amount to make the program permanent.

This approach is more likely to be successful for two reasons:

- By reducing the size of your initial request (and thus the size of the commitment), you make it easier for the audience to say yes.
- The consistency principle makes it more likely that the audience will say yes, because people want to act in ways that are consistent with how they acted previously.

As a manager, you'll constantly face the challenge of persuading people to do what you want. Perhaps you need to convince your team to accept a policy change, or maybe you want to persuade executives that your idea is better than someone else's. Mastering tactics of influence can dramatically increase your success in gaining consensus, swaying skeptics, and converting opponents.

Delivering Actionable Feedback

Managers are judged not by how well they serve executives but by how productive their teams are, and feedback might be the most powerful tool managers have to develop high-performing people. Performance is a function of a person's ability (knowledge, skills, and information) plus motivation. Assuming that a person is motivated, effective feedback will improve performance (Locke and Latham 1990).

Actionable feedback is a teaching tool, guidance that someone can learn from. It is not merely a set of observations or facts that do not suggest any need for action. It is a clear and candid evaluation of how well someone's performance is aligned with their desired career path and the organization's goals.

When feedback is delivered as part of a coaching or mentoring atmosphere, it demonstrates caring, builds trust, and presents an important gift—a manager's undivided attention—says British organizational theorist Lynda Gratton (2008). Providing an opportunity for employees to flourish and encouraging their development makes for happier people, better functioning teams, and higher-performing companies.

Feedback should not be limited to conversations between managers and direct reports. Leaders also need feedback, and that should be part of the organization's culture. A military commander who wants an accurate assessment of battlefield conditions will ask for input from numerous people. Similarly, politicians need to hear what voters think of them, coaches should know what is on players' minds, and managers need feedback from their direct reports, because as they continue to rise they become more insulated from the everyday happenings in the workplace. But while many managers consider honest, insightful input to be critical to their job, they often shield themselves from it. If managers put up barriers to two-way communication, especially when it's negative, they miss out on critical information.

"If you reduce your view of the organization to the little circle of people who tell you how great you are," a predictable downward spiral will follow, says Mike Doble (2018), a public relations director at defense contractor Raytheon. "If the company is like a battlefield, and you want to know what's going on, you want to hear from everyone," not just those who will tell you want you want to hear.

Performance Conversations Can Be Stressful

Few people would disagree that feedback is valuable, and most employees want it. In the best of circumstances, a manager will deliver their assessment respectfully, while the employee listens to or reads it and clarifies any uncertainties; then the employee implements the recommendations.

Unfortunately, critiquing a person's performance when the evaluation is not positive is rarely easy. Managers dread delivering the news, employees shrink at hearing it, and the discussion can become heated and stressful.

When an employee gets defensive, the manager often asserts their point of view more emphatically, which causes the tension to rise to the point where the employee is no longer hearing what the manager is trying to say.

If delivered properly, feedback is a gift, says Chevron's Dave Samson (2018), who is known in the communications profession to be an authentic and compassionate leader. "You have to have an outcome—usually it's enhanced performance—and be committed to their success."

Feedback discussions are more likely to be strained if managers aren't trained in how to give feedback effectively, because managers are unprepared for the psychological and emotional dynamics that can affect the atmosphere.

Here are a few tips managers should be aware of to provide feedback and avoid alienating an employee in such a conversation.

Prepare for Difficult Conversations

We are rarely at a loss for words—we chat, expound on a familiar topic, spread good news, or ask for something. But difficult conversations make us squirm because they are about contentious topics that might create conflict. Perhaps you need to settle a relationship dispute, reprimand an employee, express a disagreement with the boss, or ask the neighbor to keep her dog on a leash.

But having to address sensitive issues is part of managing. While such conversations might seem awkward at first, we have to remember that anything new requiring us to change our approach is awkward. Think about a right-handed person who breaks their right arm and suddenly has to use their left hand for almost everything. This discomfort is in part why many managers avoid these discussions. But the problem is not likely to fix itself, and ignoring it or delaying the conversation will only make the situation worse. For example, if a manager expends significant effort correcting and completing the work of a direct report who is not measuring up, that employee's poor performance will soon reflect more on the manager for failing to address the problem. While uncomfortable, a difficult conversation will help the employee perform better, which will then reflect favorably on the manager.

One reason these interactions are difficult is that our minds are abuzz with questions as we manage three streams of thought, as Douglas Stone, Bruce Patton, and Sheila Heen (1999) discuss in *Difficult Conversations:*

- When we disagree with someone about what happened, we're asking: Are their facts correct? Whose fault was it? What did they mean by what they said? What do I do now?
- We also think about our feelings: Is my point of view accurate? Are their feelings valid? What are the ramifications of this conflict?
- We also examine ourselves: Am I a bungling incompetent? Am I learning something that conflicts with my self-image? Is this an accurate reflection of me?

Holly Weeks, author of *Failure to Communicate* (2010) and a lecturer at the Harvard Kennedy School of Government, emphasizes three essential elements of communication when the situation is delicate:

- **Clarity.** Communicating with clarity means avoiding using ambiguous words and winding, circuitous sentences that leave the reader guessing at the meaning. Be explicit. Hearing the unvarnished truth allows the person to process the information, understand your position, and determine a response. Be careful about the gap between what you intended to say and what the listener or reader thinks you said. When you rely on your intentions, the burden is on the listener to decipher your meaning, but the responsibility rests with you to ensure that your meaning is clear. We might wish that the other person would realize what we mean so that we don't have to be explicit, but that forces the listener to interpret rather than forcing the speaker to communicate clearly. Each of us is responsible for clearly presenting what we mean.
- **Neutral tone.** Channel the airline's method for making flight announcements: clear and direct, expressing no emotion. Stressful conversations tax our ability to remain composed, but maintaining poise allows the receiver to pay attention to the message. Body language, such as raised eyebrows, a contorted

facial expression, or a smirk, distracts the listener, who then focuses on the delivery.

- **Temperance.** Avoid inflammatory or abrasive wording that prompts the listener or reader to feel under attack and dismiss what you're saying. Intemperate wording inflames the discussion, and, as Weeks (2018) wrote, "We're not in stressful conversations to score points or to create enemies. The goal is to advance the conversation, to hear and be heard accurately, and to have a functional exchange between two people."

Acknowledge Your Biases

When managers and direct reports sit down to discuss a performance review, each comes to the conversation with their own perception of what happened and why. This is called the actor-observer bias, and these conflicting opinions can have a dramatic impact on the employee-manager relationship. While an employee sees their behavior as a response to the situation, the manager, lacking a detailed knowledge of those factors, attributes the employee's behavior to personality traits, and "often errs by overattributing" the cause to those traits (Jones and Nisbett 1987).

Employees (actors) tend to have what psychologists call a "self-serving bias." When an outcome is successful, they tend to attribute the success to their own performance. When the outcome is a failure or is a neutral result, however, they blame external factors such as bad luck or the difficulty of the task (Miller and Ross 1975). They point to situational factors that existed at the time of the action: conflicting pressures, obstacles, or options that were unavailable to them. In addition, they are inclined to characterize their actions as inevitable, which social scientists call the "ego defense" concept. Taking credit for successes and denying responsibility for failures enables individuals to protect their self-esteem.

Managers should also be aware that most people have an unrealistically favorable view of themselves. Psychologists say that people tend to be highly aware of their strengths and considerably less aware of their weaknesses (Brown 1991). In one experiment, for example, participants performed activities and then rated themselves according to several personality dimensions; they rated themselves significantly higher than observers rated them.

This is not egotistical defensiveness. Positive illusions about the self are associated with good mental health and improved performance. Psychologist Albert Bandura (1990) says that given the difficulties of everyday life—the impediments, failures, frustrations, and inequities—people need a robust sense of personal effectiveness to persevere toward success.

Talk to Your Team Regularly

Many companies provide feedback only as part of the formal performance review process, which occurs annually or twice a year. This means that employees can easily confuse feedback with judgment and ratings, creating a culture of suspicion and fear.

Because an annual conversation brings with it an air of greater importance, more frequent, less formal conversations are more effective, says former Army Col. Pilar Ryan, a former West Point professor of leadership. "When you're doing it routinely, it takes the emotion out of it, because it's not about you; it's about the process" (Ryan 2018).

This includes talking to everyone on your team. If you spend most of your time talking with people who are strong performers, they will wonder whether you're talking to "the problem child," says Ryan. "People knew I was talking with everyone and giving them feedback. They didn't need to be assured I was talking to the people who really needed to be spoken to."

Don't be a manager whose only guidance is, "As long as you don't hear from me, you're doing all right." Compliment good work. People will not only appreciate the recognition, but also be more receptive to the complaints, if and when they come.

Don't Make It Personal

Feedback should focus on the behavior, not on the individual. When you tell employees, "You're just not getting it," they hear, "You're incompetent. You're of little value here," and might feel under attack. In threatening situations, organizations, groups, and individuals tend to behave rigidly, which hinders their information processing, because they use fewer communication channels to absorb the details and respond (Staw, Sandelands, and Dutton 1981).

When giving feedback, use "I" more than "you." This will sound less pointed and less accusatory. If employees hear comments that leave them questioning their ability, self-worth, and future with the organization, they take it personally. When they're focusing on themselves rather than their performance, the feedback hinders their development.

Remember to stay focused on the facts and avoid anger and other emotions. Don't let negative opinions about the person taint the conversation and don't exaggerate. If you say you had to repeatedly correct someone when it only happened twice, it will prompt the person to doubt anything you say.

When you are discussing a work incident, don't assume anything. Make sure you know the specifics of what happened, when, where, and why. You need context. If you have data, don't draw inferences from them. Present the data and ask questions. Rather than say, "You should have included me in the discussion," try, "In the future, I would like to be part of the discussion."

Convey Constructive Feedback Via Email

Difficult conversations are not restricted to face-to-face encounters. Managers often need to discuss delicate topics in writing to continue the discussion with the other person, to update people about the details of the issue, or to document the ongoing communication for legal reasons. Sensitive topics may also be discussed in writing because people want to avoid meeting face-to-face when they are uncomfortable having such conversations.

It is important to remember that when delicate topics are discussed in writing, we should conduct ourselves as if we were facing the person. This is not only because writing is permanent and can embarrass us later, but also because self-discipline and empathy are important to our credibility.

Here is an original email that Erin fired off to Brad in response to an email he sent her team:

Hi Brad,

I was extremely surprised, and frankly put off by your email to people listing numerous action items that you want people to deal with to prepare for the WorldExpo. The management of this event is my responsibility, as marketing manager, because it is an event for customers, and the funding is coming out of the marketing budget. Having two people manage the process creates confusion and duplication.

I met with the team yesterday to discuss our strategic messages, the invitation list, and other details. You didn't attend and didn't even respond to the email announcing the meeting. If you had taken the time to look at it you would have seen that I already explained the action items you listed.

Regards,
Erin

Notice how Erin's email takes a defensive and accusational tone from the start. The first paragraph accomplishes very little besides allowing Erin to chastise Brad. Here is a possible revision:

Hi Brad,

I know that we both want to ensure that the WorldExpo is a huge success, and one way to do that is to provide everyone with a clear list of action items to avoid confusion.

Given that this is an event for customers, the planning falls on our shoulders in marketing because the funding is coming from the marketing budget. So I am working closely with my team. We discussed the strategic messages, the invitation list, and other details in a meeting yesterday, and they are clear on what they need to do.

If you have additional suggestions, please send them along, and I will be happy to consider them. I am always open to new ideas.

Regards,
Erin

Here are a few key distinctions in the revised version:

- It is calm and professional and does not put the reader on the defensive. It invites the reader in by appealing to something the reader already agrees with.
- The tone throughout the message is respectful and remains focused on the facts.
- It does not sound territorial with such comments as, "The management of this event is my responsibility." Don't make it a turf battle.
- It doesn't mention that Brad didn't attend the meeting or read the message because those issues are irrelevant. Saying "you didn't attend" or "if you had taken the time to look at it" has a parenting tone, which only serves to humiliate the person.
- The revised version has the relationship in mind. After all, Erin needs to continue working with Brad, so what is the best way to make the point while still looking ahead and moving on?
- Erin is polite and professional in saying that Brad is welcome to send her suggestions in the future. She does not guarantee that she will use them, but she keeps the door open to collaboration.

When approaching a difficult conversation, here are a few additional ways to avoid escalating a situation:

- Do not write when you are annoyed. If you do, write the message without putting an email address in the "to" box. Then let it sit in your drafts folder and look at it again the next day.
- Open with neutral information but don't take too long to reach the main point. Readers will become annoyed if you intentionally delay the disappointing news.
- Give details explaining why a decision was made or why something unpleasant needs to happen.
- Avoid inflammatory language such as *failure, mistake, sloppy,* or *what were you thinking?*
- Always treat the reader with respect, because that is what the audience will remember. Tone can affect your credibility.

Conversations can be uncomfortable, particularly when the relationship is already strained. But maintaining your composure, being candid, and avoiding putting the other person on the defensive should keep the other person engaged and lead to a productive conversation.

Be Specific

Rich feedback is detailed and descriptive. So it's important that the listener or reader understands your intended meaning. A comment to direct reports such as "you're not reliable" could mean anything. Are they late for meetings? Do they not finish projects on time? Do they fail to follow through on commitments? Too often, performance feedback is not useful for its intended purpose, in part because it is too vague for the recipient to interpret correctly.

Being specific helps set clear expectations so that people know what you need from them. It is not enough to simply tell someone, "That's not what I had in mind. Try again." If you don't provide clear guidance, the person is likely to repeat the same mistakes. Being clear about what you need from people helps to establish a path to the future.

You should also avoid ambiguous words that invite misinterpretation. Instead use examples, comparisons, and detailed explanations to help team members understand your comments.

In addition, don't practice one-way communication with vague direction: Avoid what one manager in the defense industry calls "fire and forget."

"Self-guided missiles will reach the target by themselves, but leaders can't just send a signal out," says Mike Doble (2018), director of public relations at Raytheon. "Managers feel better because they've done it," but such feedback has little chance of success because "the employee is left to figure it out."

That kind of communication amounts to "telling," but not communicating, because the manager did not connect with anyone.

Hone Your Listening Skills

We live in an age of interruptions. We stop what we're doing to answer the phone, check email, or respond to a text message; and because we cannot resist the temptation to be social, we then divert our attention to swipe through our social media feeds. The frenetic pace in many organizations today and the impact that gadgets have on the brain makes it increasingly difficult to have the discipline needed to listen carefully. How many times have we heard about problems that resulted from someone not hearing something or someone misinterpreting words? As a manager, failing to listen closely to your direct reports—in and out of feedback situations—can lead you to jump to conclusions about performance issues, and frustration on their part if they feel ignored.

Lacking good listening skills, people commit what Larry Barker and Kittie W. Watson (2000) list as the most irritating listening habits: interrupting the speaker, showing interest in something other than the conversation, rushing the speaker and making them think they're wasting the listener's time, getting ahead of the speaker and finishing their thoughts, or topping the speaker's story with "That reminds me . . . " or "That's nothing, let me tell you about . . . "

One reason is that while we speak at about 125 words per minute, our brain processes what we're hearing at about 400 words a minute. So when you listen to someone, you get way ahead of the speaker, which leaves you ample time to drift off and think about your next meeting or your to-do list.

Here are some tips for effective listening.

Keep an Open Mind

Rather than focusing on your own opinions and priorities, put yourself in the other person's position, sharing their thoughts and feelings. To do this you must be nonjudgmental, which might be why empathic listening is most closely linked to improving relationships. Don't prejudge the situation or the speaker by assuming you know what the person will say, how the situation should be handled, or that the speaker is uninformed or tends to exaggerate.

Understand the Person's Position Before Responding

When a speaker finishes—sometimes even when they just pause—listeners often respond quickly without hearing all the information. First, paraphrase your understanding of what you just heard. You don't have to begin with, "What I hear you saying is . . . " because that might sound like a stock, textbook response. But you can ask, "Are you saying . . . ?" Or you could make it a statement: "So, you're saying . . . "

Show You Are Engaged

Be patient and present. Some people get impatient listening to speakers they don't think are as smart as they are or who don't seem to have coherent ideas. Maintain eye contact and show interest by nodding or saying "I understand" or "uh-huh." We usually have congestion in our minds. As we listen, related thoughts, possible solutions, questions, details, and unrelated urgent issues will pop into our brain and compete for attention. Staying focused is difficult.

Don't Try to Remember Every Detail

It is impossible to listen to someone and memorize all the facts because while you are trying to memorize one fact, you will miss another, wrote Ralph Nichols and Leonard Stevens in *Harvard Business Review* (1957). You will see the trees but miss the forest. Instead, remembering the bigger picture will help you remember more facts supporting that idea than trying to memorize all the facts.

Don't Interrupt

When we are processing information and a question occurs to us, we often blurt it out, interrupting the speaker's train of thought. Or when we assume we know what a speaker will say or what they are thinking, we step in when they pause and finish their thought. Exercise restraint and let the person finish. Don't monopolize the conversation by talking too much about yourself.

Change Your Own Behavior Patterns

Trying to jump in with a solution to a problem rarely works in any relationship, business or personal, so avoid being "Mr. fix-it" if the speaker just wants an ear to listen. Start with not creating a response while the other person is still talking; this is a sign you are not hearing what they are saying.

Many managers are surprised to learn that others consider them to be poor listeners, so commit to improving your communication skills, especially given their importance.

Invite Input by Asking Questions

You often can make your point effectively—sometimes more so—by posing a question rather than being direct. If someone is not doing an effective job leading a project and you sit down to discuss the lack of progress, first ask the person what is going well. Then, rather than asking, "What isn't going well?" ask, "What do you think needs improvement?"

Try the stop, start, continue approach:

- Is there anything I do now that you want me to stop doing?
- Is there anything I don't do now that you want me to start doing?
- Is there anything I do now that you want me to continue doing?

For example, you also might ask, "What can I do to make your job easier?" or "How can I improve the way I give feedback so that we both understand the goal and the best way to achieve it?"

Or instead of telling an employee that they need to use a different method, try asking, "Do you think it would be faster and easier if you did X?" By allowing the person to answer, and maybe to add other ideas, they feel as if they have contributed to the solution and thus retain a sense of ownership.

A core principle of journalistic writing is to paint pictures for the reader. But when Associated Press Bureau Chief Jon Kellogg saw an obscure word in a writer's draft, he did not simply hand it to the writer and tell him to write more clearly. He asked the writer, "Can you draw me a picture of a synergy?" The writer didn't need to answer; he knew instantly what he needed to change, without being on the receiving end of humiliating criticism.

Manage Your Expectations

Jean-Francois Manzoni, dean of the International Institute for Management Development, says many managers contribute to a person's under-performance. He and his colleague Jean-Louis Barsoux call it "the set-up to fail syndrome," a dynamic in which employees who are perceived to be weaker achievers perform down to the manager's expectations.

Here is how the syndrome develops: A manager deems a person's performance to be subpar, so to boost performance they focus more attention on the employee. They watch the employee more closely at meetings, require them to get approval before making decisions, and ask them to provide more facts and details to justify their decisions.

The employee, interpreting the increased supervision as a lack of trust, might begin to doubt their own ability and become nervous and hesitant about making decisions. The manager views that as poor performance and increases the supervision. To avoid criticism, the employee withdraws and stops making meaningful contributions. And the downward spiral continues.

It is extremely difficult to reverse the set-up-to-fail syndrome, so Manzoni urges managers to adopt a coaching approach. The manager and employee should have early conversations and agree on the expectations of the role. Continual feedback on performance can assist in creating a far healthier dynamic where both parties have continual dialogue, maintain mutual respect, and keep the employee separated from the performance.

Running Effective Team Meetings

When was the last time you heard anyone say, "Terrific! I have another meeting to go to. Looking forward to it." If you so much as mention the word *meeting* to most businesspeople, you'll elicit an eyeroll or a cynical smirk.

There are good reasons to have meetings, of course, such as sharing ideas, inviting feedback, promoting collaboration, providing guidance, and reaching decisions. In person or virtually, meetings should be important tools to draw on everyone's expertise, solve problems, manage productivity—and generally communicate with your team.

Instead, people dread meetings, which continue to dominate as a form of communication, overwhelming the schedules of managers and direct reports alike. The feeling of dread is due to the nature of meetings today— they are so often unproductive and boring. They have also been known to raise anxiety among workers who worry that the waste of time is hindering their performance.

So while you may view a meeting as the perfect opportunity to get everyone together, share crucial information, and bond as a team, be aware that you might be unwittingly hindering your direct reports' performance. And this extends to people outside your team who invite your direct reports to meetings—it's your job as the manager to step in and decide whether they truly need to go. By doing so, you become their advocate, freeing up their time to finish a project on deadline or pursue a development opportunity.

When you're the one running the meeting, there are a few factors to consider to get the most out of it.

Do the Advance Work

First, be sure a meeting is necessary. This means respecting everyone's time. One reason people resent meetings is that they often deal with issues that could be handled over email, phone, or a conversation in the cafeteria. If you haven't given thought about what you want to accomplish, it's likely you're jumping the gun by scheduling a meeting. Ask yourself: Are you looking for input? Do you want to share new information? Do you want the group to make a decision? Only once you've answered these questions will you know whether a meeting is the right way to communicate with your team.

Another snafu that managers, especially new ones, make is not being judicious enough about who should attend the meeting. Say, you've got some information that's relevant to half your team, but more of nice-to-know for the other half. So, in an effort to avoid keeping some people in the dark, you invite everyone. Well, think about how those who didn't need to know will feel about going to that 30-minute or hourlong meeting. You're wasting their time! That's surely what they're thinking to themselves. Instead, consider inviting only the need-to-know staff and sending a recap email after the meeting on which you copy the rest of the team. This relates to recurring meetings as well. Don't keep inviting the same people just because they attended the first one—assess whether they need to attend each week. Remember, keep the group small for best results—large groups can lead to tangled discussions and needless, irrelevant chatter.

Once you've decided whether you need a meeting and have whittled down the attendee list, set and distribute an agenda before the meeting. This signals to your staff that you've put forethought into it and what you hope to accomplish. They'll also know they need to come prepared. Ask people whose support you might need if they have suggestions, if they think anything is missing from the agenda, or if there are issues they want the group to discuss. Is there anything on the agenda that might spark resistance or irritation? Having this identified before the meeting will help save time, because it helps build relationships and can avoid surprises.

Consider a situation where a manager drags three members of her team away from their work to go over how to fix a problem on a high-profile project. Without an agenda, she spends the first 15 minutes catching everyone up to speed and laying out the goals for the meeting. Then she asks one member for a status report, but this person didn't realize he needed to pull numbers from the data tracker. So he opens his laptop and, after five minutes, casts his screen to the rest of the group.

Now imagine being in a meeting full of these unwelcome surprises, one after the other. Not only did the manager waste precious time overviewing the meeting's purpose and scrambling for information, but by doing so she also implied that being unprepared when choosing to communicate within the organization is OK.

When creating an agenda, make sure to clearly state the purpose of the meeting (to make a decision, elicit ideas, and so on). List the agenda items as well as the outcome you want (such as *Off-site meeting: Need agreement on agenda*), which keeps the discussion tight and focused. Next, tell people about any topics you want them to think about ahead of time. You can also ask them to come prepared with solutions to problems, which will help reduce discussion time.

Keep the Meeting Flowing

It's OK to open a meeting with a quick summary of the meeting's purpose— just keep it brief. You can open by presenting the major items and the outcome you are hoping for, as well as mentioning how the agenda topics are tied to larger goals.

Once the meeting has started, you need to create the right atmosphere. People need to feel secure enough to speak up if they do not understand or if they want to challenge someone on a point. Attendees should know that you want them to participate and that they can be candid and tactfully direct. Be sure everyone has a chance to speak.

That said, your role as a manager often extends to controlling the discussion. While creating an open, free-wheeling atmosphere may seem like the best way to show you're not an autocrat, you still need to run meetings that adhere to the agenda. Invite everyone to express themselves and to share their expertise, but keep the discussion focused. Here are some things speakers often do that they should stay away from:

- Drift off topic.
- Make points about the topic that are only marginally relevant.
- Discuss a specific problem that affects only them.
- Promote their agenda.

There's nothing wrong with politely, yet forcefully, interjecting when someone is leading the group astray. In fact, your team will respect you for it—and thank you for tightening up everyone's communication style.

If the purpose of your meeting is to make a series of decisions, move on once there's a consensus. Meeting participants will appreciate that you're sticking to the agenda and trying to end on time. Empower your team members to speak up about the time if a discussion becomes prolonged. Too often, discussions drag on because people feel a need to say something, even though they are only repeating what others have said. Ask people to contribute information that no one has put forth.

Being a good manager requires that you recognize the different communication preferences of your team members during meetings. Although you want full group participation, recognize that introverts would rather not play a central role in the discussion. They are uncomfortable being the center of attention, listen more than they talk, are more analytical, dislike conflict, and often do their best work alone. If they want to contribute, they will. But you also need to be aware of any extroverts who dominate the conversation. Just because one person seems to be speaking up more than the others doesn't mean they're trying to be rude or are even cognizant of their behavior. It's your job to ensure that the *opportunity* to contribute is available to everyone. As your team becomes more comfortable, you'll need to learn how best to ensure communication flows equitably.

The best way to end a meeting is on time, with a recap. Too often, meetings end with everyone dashing off to their other work—or perhaps another meeting. Failing to debrief means the group departs without closure or a clear direction of how to proceed. Mention the important things the group decided on, and repeat what people need to do in the days ahead.

Follow Up on Meeting Action Items

After the meeting is over and everyone's back at their desks, send a summary of what was discussed and any action items. Don't assume that action will be taken because you ended the meeting with a recap.

Talk to people whose support you need to ask how the meeting went and if there's anything they would like you to know that they didn't want to discuss in the meeting. While good managers are trusted by their direct reports, there will still be times when people don't feel comfortable voicing an opinion in front of the group. By following up individually with the meeting participants, you ensure you capture all spoken and unspoken thoughts.

Finally, as a manager, your direct reports notice your actions, which in turn influences how they think they should act. If you've communicated to someone that you'd send them information, send it. If you promised you'd perform some task, do it. Failing to deliver on guarantees you've committed to will reduce the trust you're hoping to build with your team.

Conclusion

Managers who lack strong communication skills are unlikely to succeed, given the percentage of time they spend communicating, and the role of communication in achieving corporate goals. By having superior writing, speaking, and listening skills, and by being transparent, managers can inform, guide, and motivate employees to achieve goals. They can foster relationships, build trust, and influence those around them.

To build credibility, effective communicators need to connect with employees. They talk their language, simplify the complex, and invest time to understand their perspective. They make them know they care.

Underpinning all these skills is the deft use of language. It plays a role in every situation in which a manager tries to inform or persuade: email, formal memos, performance feedback, reports, proposals, and presentations to senior leaders. Through the careful use of words, tone, and simplicity, managers communicate the organization's vision, facilitate change, and connect employees to the strategy.

No longer a "soft skill," management communication is critical to an organization's business performance in the 21st century. Whereas organizational communication was traditionally top-down and carefully controlled by the sender, today it is widely distributed, interactive, and focused on the recipient. Improving communication skill requires work, but it is worth the effort because it can be a differentiator in your career.

3

Collaboration

<><><><><><><><><><><><><><><><><><><><><><><><><><><><><><><><><><><><><><><><><><><><><><><><><><><>

Winsor Jenkins

My passion for leadership and talent development began early in my career, when I was introduced to leadership guru Ken Blanchard and several of his programs and books. After that, I was hooked. Over the years, I learned as much as I could about leaders who were successful not only in the business world, but in other arenas such as politics, sports, and even on the battlefield. Learning these lessons from people like Nelson Mandela, Ernest Shackleton, Colin Powell, John Wooden, and others was important to me because they demonstrated real leadership in the field.

My favorite leader is Nelson Mandela. He was an optimist with a vision for replacing apartheid with democracy in South Africa. During his 27 years in prison, he planned how he would accomplish that task, using persuasion over violence to create a win-win solution and change a nation. He was also an innovative leader who saw the value of sport to leverage peoples' emotions, demonstrating a collaborative mindset in winning people to his cause.

Throughout my career I've spent most of my time working with, developing, and coaching leaders. Serving in multiple roles in human resources (including vice president of human resources at my last company), I often found myself in situations where I was constantly trying to persuade people to move from win-lose scenarios to win-win scenarios. While I never kept score on how well I did in achieving win-win solutions, I can say there was plenty of room for improvement.

At some point, I decided to improve my scoring tactics for generating win-win solutions, as a result, I wrote *The Collaborator*. In this book, I married my passion for leadership with my passion for sport, introducing people to a new, innovative way to collaborate and produce win-win outcomes.

This chapter is about how management innovation leads to a new way to practice genuine team collaboration in the workplace. We all know and recognize product innovation as the kind of innovation that captures the headlines. Yet, management innovation matters most and is rarely mentioned as an option for creating a competitive advantage. The problem is, we don't know how to collaborate to produce win-win outcomes in a world that promotes individual performance over team performance; this inevitably results in win-lose outcomes. Look around and you will see people (and cultures) with values that promote individual responsibility and performance over team performance. Just as "good is the enemy of great," could it be that individual values are the enemy of organizational values, such as teamwork?

As you start your learning journey to become a collaborative manager, my hope is that the material covered in this chapter inspires you to change your approach to collaboration. Your team's success depends upon it. This will take a commitment to lead with a collaboration mindset and manage using competencies focused on collaboration. Like Nelson Mandela, you will also need to leverage your leadership to win people to your cause and produce win-win outcomes.

I've elected to focus this chapter on how first-time managers can collaborate to win. In doing so, I also hope to provide them with insights for how to coach the people on their teams. Indeed, an effective approach to collaboration requires a coaching mindset for developing talent.

In this chapter, I provide a clear path (a new management process) for you to follow as you develop a team that practices genuine team collaboration. While this learning journey may not take you places where no one has gone before, it will be a journey on a road less traveled. Along this journey, you will:

- Discover a new operating platform or model that helps you transition from top-down, chain-of-command thinking that promotes dependency to a mindset that views interdependence as the key to winning.

- Learn an alternative mindset for practicing genuine collaborative teamwork. Composed of a series of operating principles that help your team collaborate, this mindset will illuminate why it's important to lead with the goal of producing win-win outcomes.

- Develop a new skill set focused on collaboration competencies. Combined with collaboration operating principles, this skill set will provide a practical method to achieve genuine team collaboration in the workplace, leading to improved team effectiveness and win-win outcomes.

- Understand what it takes to practice genuine team collaboration through the eyes of a team coach. That way, you get an outside-in and inside-out understanding of team collaboration. This will make you not only a better collaborator, but a better team coach.

- Gain a renewed appreciation for team coaching and why it's a critical skill set for you to learn and apply as a team manager. Without it, team performance will suffer and talent development will suffer, too.

In looking to understand current realities and future challenges, I've gone to the past, blending old theory with new thinking. I hope this serves as a building block for kick-starting a frontline manager's understanding of what it means to practice genuine collaboration on the job.

Cracking the Collaboration Code

◇◇◇

Down, But Not Out

Toni was apprehensive about how she would effectively lead a team of eight people scattered around the world. Dealing with multicultural differences—along with managing others—was a completely new set of challenges for her. On top of that, her new boss was asking her to learn and apply a new model for managing her team. He was convinced that this represented the most appropriate model for managing people and teams in today's global business world. He believed that learning and applying this model, which used a collaborative mindset, would be critical to her success.

"To tell you the truth," she said to her husband that night, "I'm having second thoughts about taking on this new job. My boss and I met today to discuss how we're going to make this work. What if I can't live up to his expectations?"

Toni was honored her boss thought so highly of her. At the same time, however, she didn't want him to regret his decision to promote her. Although her goal was to become a manager, she was feeling a little overwhelmed. She wanted the challenge of managing others but hadn't expected her first management role to be on a global level. What did that even look like? She knew that her eagerness to learn and her strong work ethic would carry her only so far in her new assignment. She had made numerous personal sacrifices to earn her degree, become a talented engineer, and position herself for the opportunity to manage people. Failing in her new job was not an option.

Winning Team Collaboration Starts With You

You're a manager, perhaps leading others for the first time. You've been successful in the past. Perhaps you were the best at what you did as an individual contributor in your organization. Or you were sought out for a leadership role based on your ability to work with others to achieve results at the department, unit, or division level.

Taking on a new management role is challenging. It takes competence, commitment, and courage. We all want to be successful and yet much can go wrong when we take on new responsibilities—for ourselves, our employees, and our companies. Managing change can be unnerving to say the least.

Most people struggle in their first managerial role. Why? It could be tied to a lack of resources provided by the organization in the form of management training and ongoing coaching. It may be a lack of self-awareness; that is, you may be someone who doesn't understand how your motivations, values, and underlying assumptions affect your behavior as you attempt to lead your team. Finally, you may simply be reluctant to learn and grow as a manager.

As a new manager of a team, you will be charged with the task of creating a collaborative environment or culture that leverages the team's resources for achieving a competitive advantage. This includes building trust inside the team, understanding the human dynamics of team formulation and ongoing maintenance, maintaining productive relationships, identifying team roles, and setting and communicating team goals. Your challenge includes coaching the members of your team when needed.

Managing in the Age of Collaboration

Today's business world is a highly competitive global economy where technology enables people to be more responsive to markets, empowering those on the front line to make decisions, take risks, and manage constant change. And with more and more work being done by teams, organizations require a new operating platform to help people develop and apply a mindset based on interdependence versus a mindset based on chain of command.

The need to change how we operate our organizations to better match up with all the challenges presented in the global economy has been echoed in the past by numerous management thinkers including Ken Blanchard and Gary Hamel. This also includes Stephen R. Covey, who made it clear that the chain of command mindset still dominating today's workplace does not work in our new economy, where interconnectedness is changing the world.

As teams continue to grow, collaboration will be seen as the key to organizational success. The ability to deal with today's realities demands the application of a collaborative mindset that can harness the power of connection across the team's network to produce innovative solutions. In *The Collaborator*, I compared our highly competitive global business world to soccer, another environment where people on the team must effectively collaborate. Played at its highest level, soccer is a great example of a sport with teams whose success is directly related to their ability to apply a collaborative mindset, recognizing the interdependency between players on the field. In soccer, players must be technically skilled and able to multitask, assimilate new information on the run, adapt to changing conditions, and apply multiple skills across a network to achieve results.

◇◇◇

The Pitch for a New Operating Platform

In the 1800s, Great Britain promoted organized team sports like soccer to help educate and prepare people to participate in the British Empire's global affairs. In his book, *Physical Education in England Since 1800,* author Peter McIntosh wrote that organized games were promoted to meet social needs, develop character, and teach loyalty, self-sacrifice, cooperation, and the like. McIntosh concluded that public education was being consciously connected to success on the Empire's battlefields.

Did Great Britain's attempt to perpetuate its influence throughout the world by promoting organized games like soccer represent the first attempt to manage globally? Can soccer provide a more realistic model or operational platform to help people transition from top-down, chain-of-command thinking that promotes dependency to a mindset that views interdependence as the key to winning in today's highly competitive global world? Without question, the parallels are striking.

◇◇◇

What Is Collaboration?

Like the topic of culture, collaboration is always at risk of being oversimplified. Collaborating effectively is not as simple as saying, "Let's cooperate with each other." Practicing genuine team collaboration is much more complex and challenging.

In the 2016 research report *ACCEL: The Skills That Make a Winning Manager,* the Association for Talent Development defined collaboration as:

> *Creating an environment and culture of teamwork (in this case, the team comprises the manager and direct reports). Managers who excel in this skill foster trust and relationships between all team members, clarify team roles, and encourage cooperation toward achieving a common goal (OPM 1997). By encouraging trust and relationship building between team members, direct reports can share knowledge with and learn from one another.*

We know that collaboration is used to describe how organizations leverage people to deal with the accelerating—and unprecedented—levels of change today. In this VUCA (volatile, uncertain, complex, and ambiguous) world, collaboration was rated by CEOs in IBM's 2012 global CEO study, *Leading Through Connections,* as the number one professional skill needed to be successful in a more interconnected environment. As Bruce Griffiths argues, a collaborative mindset is no longer a "nice-to-have," it's a "need-to-have" to make sure you're able to understand and adapt to constant change.

We also know the importance of developing the infrastructure; that is, developing an operating platform that supports a collaborative culture—before developing actual collaboration skills—as pointed out by CEOs in the 2013 IBM global C-suite study, *The Customer-Activated Enterprise.* This includes knowing that psychological safety is a critical driver to make a team work well. We cannot assume that managers and their direct reports will simply collaborate well.

Furthermore, we know that most people don't function with a mindset that supports the skill set to effectively collaborate in the workplace. The typical mindset supports what we call group work, described as cooperating and coordinating with others. Because it's not in our DNA, the idea that people can flip mindsets on demand, like hitting a switch, is not realistic. This disconnect explains, in part, why developing teams that effectively collaborate has been an ongoing challenge in organizations.

May the Best Team Win

As a young boy growing up and playing sports, I often heard these words just before the start of a game: "May the best team win!" Looking back, it was a phrase that had a limited meaning. After all, we had heard them numerous times each summer. We expected to hear it as if it were just part of the coin-flip ritual to see which team would get the ball. I would have never imagined how that phrase could have real meaning in today's global business world.

Back in the day, the idea that teamwork meant collaboration did not come up, except perhaps in the case of crisis. And the term *interdependent* was not a word I was familiar with. In fact, *collaboration* had more of a negative connotation, often described in the context of collaborating with the enemy. Why? We all grew up with values that favored individual responsibility and performance over team performance. This was played out in society, at school, at work, and anywhere else we competed against one another as independent parts of the system.

Here's the good news: Genuine collaboration can be learned. It starts with practice and training, followed by ongoing coaching. In today's business world, the phrase "may the best team win" will have real meaning for organizations that are serious about leveraging resources. Again, if the name of the game is innovation for business growth, the stakes are always high. (Use the Your Preference for Collaboration? tool in the appendix to assess your preference.)

Mindset and Skill Set

Collaboration is part mindset, part skill set. Both components are necessary for practicing genuine collaborative teamwork. The mindset recognizes a mutual dependency—or interdependency—between people on the team. Without that recognition, there cannot be true collaboration. The skill set consists of a series of competencies focused on collaboration. Developing mindset before skill set is the key to unlocking the collaboration code.

The collaboration mindset is made up of 11 operating principles that serve as the foundation for developing a new way of thinking. These operating principles, adapted from the global game of soccer to mirror the team's actions on the field, serve as governing principles to help frame individual and team decisions around collaboration—and ultimately habits and behaviors—leading to improved team effectiveness. Without these principles (and the corresponding platform described in Figure 3-1), the team's actions and their application of tools will be limited.

Figure 3-1. Collaboration Operating Principles and Competency Components

Operating Principles	Competencies
Focus on Team, Not Position	Change Agility, Learning Agility
Understand That Everyone Can Play	Drive and Energy, Initiative, Technical Expertise
Embrace Diversity	Global Skills, Relationship Building, Sensitivity
Rely on One Another	Relationship Building, Team Management, Team Player
Promote Individual and Team Values	Global Skills, Integrity, Relationship Building, Sensitivity
Seek Skillful, Adaptable Players	Change Agility, Learning Agility, Organizing and Planning
Charge the Team to Perform the Work	Results Orientation, Visioning
Empower Players to Win	Problem Solving and Decision Making, and Risk Taking
Coach Teams to Respond to Changing Conditions on Their Own	Change Agility, Problem Solving and Decision Making, Communicativeness
Develop Partners on the Field	Communicativeness, Coaching and Counseling, Delegation, Influence, Relationship Building
Achieve Cross-Cultural Agility	Global Skills, Learning Agility, Relationship Building, Self-Objectivity

When these operating principles and competencies are combined, they form the collaboration operating platform, which, embedded in the team's charter, can help the team leverage their efforts, such as plan work, understand roles, set direction, and integrate and orient new members to the team. (The Collaboration Operating Platform tool in the appendix offers detailed descriptions of the principles and competencies.)

What Makes a Winning Collaborative Team Manager?

Give Up Some Control

Pondering over his next move, Tim realized that he would have to deal with Kurt, one of his top production technicians who had been promoted three months earlier to a frontline managerial role overseeing a key production line. Kurt had been an excellent technician before getting promoted. He was also loyal and dedicated to the company, often working extra hours if needed.

However, Tim was also being approached by many of Kurt's production people in the plant cafeteria, who all shared the same feedback: that Kurt was always telling them what to do. Some described it as badgering, others were getting frustrated, and a few were ready to quit. They all said that his behavior was making them feel like they were not trusted to get the job done. Everyone seemed to like Kurt, but his credibility as a manager was slipping.

Tim decided to use this situation as a coaching opportunity—a time to redirect Kurt. As the operations manager, Tim had seen this pattern of behavior in other new managers, so he was confident that he could coach him. Kurt needed to learn how to use a variety of managerial styles to support his people; he also needed to understand that telling everyone what to do all the time was not productive. Kurt was over-supervising his people, suppressing collaboration.

Tim knew that while the crew's production numbers were good now, they would not be sustainable in the long term if Kurt's behavior did not change. Not only did Kurt need to understand the value in "delegating" production to his crew (which happened to be highly experienced), he also needed to understand that the "crew's" perception of how he managed was more important than his own perception.

Kurt, meanwhile, was feeling like things were going well in his new role. So he was curious when Tim asked him to stop by his office at the end of the day.

"What's up?" Kurt asked, walking into Tim's office.

Develop Self-Awareness

To collaborate effectively, managers need to develop their self-awareness. In fact, managers who don't succeed typically lack self-awareness. Author Daniel Goleman and associates (2002) have made this proposition highly visible over the past 20 years by showing the significance of emotional intelligence (EQ) to developing managers. In fact, decades of research now point to EQ as the critical factor that sets high-performing managers apart from others.

According to Goleman's model, high-performing managers have the capacity for recognizing their own feelings and those of others, motivating themselves, practicing reflection as needed, and understanding and working on their strengths and weaknesses. Their end game is to reduce blind spots that show up and interfere with their performance. His EQ model describes four domains, or clusters: self-awareness, self-management, social awareness, and relationship management. Each one includes competencies that can be used to develop EQ (Figure 3-2). Note, research also supports that self-awareness is a necessary underpinning of both self-management and social awareness.

As an aspiring high-performing manager, your path for successful collaboration starts by identifying and tackling blind spots that typically show up in the form of interpersonal competencies, such as delegation. Because you may not be aware of them and their impact in your new role, you must be open to continuous feedback, learning, and coaching. This includes taking responsibility and accountability for your actions, changing thinking patterns, altering behavior and trying new things, revising responses to feelings as needed, and the like.

Figure 3-2. EQ's Four Domains and Competencies

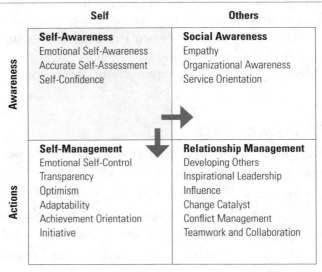

	Self	Others
Awareness	**Self-Awareness** Emotional Self-Awareness Accurate Self-Assessment Self-Confidence	**Social Awareness** Empathy Organizational Awareness Service Orientation
Actions	**Self-Management** Emotional Self-Control Transparency Optimism Adaptability Achievement Orientation Initiative	**Relationship Management** Developing Others Inspirational Leadership Influence Change Catalyst Conflict Management Teamwork and Collaboration

Adapted from Goleman, Boyatis, and McKee (2002).

You can begin building self-awareness by understanding how your motivations, values, and underlying assumptions affect your behavior—and the team's performance. This also includes understanding how to motivate other people. For example, understanding what worked as a motivator for you in the past likely won't work to motivate others. The first-time manager needs to understand the need to value the contributions of others on the team. But *motivation* is a word that has come to mean all things to all people. Most people view motivation like they view quality: they can't define it, but they know it when they see it! For most of us, motivation represents a gray area. It's an energy that, once seen or experienced, is perhaps the ultimate intangible in helping individuals, teams, and organizations achieve results. Building self-awareness takes time and commitment, but without it, you'll struggle to find the balance for collaboration within your team that values the contributions of everyone.

Taking on a new frontline manager role also requires learning a new skill set. For example, getting the understanding and buy-in to let go of past assumptions around what made you successful as a professional—for example as an engineer, accountant, or technical expert—is often challenging, especially in the case of someone perceived as a star performer. At the same time, it's important to recognize the value in retaining and leveraging your technical and functional expertise. Bruce Griffiths has made this point clear by describing the importance of this expertise for generating personal power to help leverage your leadership agenda with your team.

Demonstrating flexibility in your management style represents another important part of your skill set for building self-awareness. The idea that a single style of collaboration such as directing, can be applied to all situations to manage both individuals and teams is not effective. Because leadership is an influence process, managing your team will require you to apply diverse management or motivational styles to achieve success in your role.

Understanding why relationship building is important to your success as a first-time manager is also critical in building your self-awareness. Placing an emphasis on relationship building creates a very demanding position for many people who are first-time managers. Why? Technology continues making it easier to avoid the interpersonal, face-to-face communication so important to establishing and maintaining relationships. Yet we all know a team manager or team coach whose success is totally dependent upon their ability to transcend technique (including technology) and deal with people on a relationship basis to achieve results. As I like to say to managers I work with, you can't technique people to death using a newly acquired tool or technology! They won't let you. Management, then, is not just a matter of acquired expertise. Management (leadership) is first about relationships and relationship building, to paraphrase leadership guru Warren Bennis.

Check Your Underlying Assumptions

Where do you stand when it comes to your underlying assumptions or beliefs about the potential of people to get the job done? Management professor Douglas McGregor (1960) introduced the world to "Theory X and Theory Y" in his book, *The Human Side of Enterprise.* His theory deals with underlying assumptions people and organizations bring to the table, and how those assumptions influence the task of managing people. In this case, Theory X assumptions are described as negative assumptions about people, and Theory Y assumptions as positive assumptions about people (Figure 3-3).

It is critical for you to understand your assumptions as you start your learning journey to become a collaborative manager. For example, do you believe in the potential of people to get the job done? If yes, you may be described as a Theory Y leader, well positioned to leverage your assumptions to encourage collaboration and innovation.

Figure 3-3. Theory X and Theory Y

Theory X	Theory Y
» People inherently dislike work and will avoid it if they can. » People must be coerced, controlled, directed, and threatened to make them work. » The average human being prefers to be directed, wishes to avoid responsibility, and has relatively little ambition.	» The expenditure of physical and mental effort in work is as natural as play or rest. » People can exercise self-direction and self-control in the service of objectives to which they are committed. » The average human being learns, under proper conditions, not only to accept but to seek responsibility.

Adapted from McGregor (1960).

When talking about Theory X and Theory Y, I often share the story about New United Motors Manufacturing Inc. (NUMMI) to reinforce the significance of underlying assumptions on worker behavior and performance. I think it's one of the best stories to describe the consequences of using Theory X versus Theory Y assumptions in the workplace. Here's a condensed version of the story:

In the mid-1980s, Toyota and GM established the joint venture NUMMI in Fremont, California. The goal was to reopen a former GM plant—which had been considered the worst workforce in the U.S. automobile industry because of its frequent strikes, intentional sabotage, and high absenteeism rates—and create high-quality products at low cost by implementing the Toyota Way. Contrary to GM's application of Theory X assumptions, the Toyota Way represented a system where respect for people was a key tenet in finding problems and making improvements (Theory Y assumptions). By changing the plant's culture to one built on mutual trust, Toyota was able to turn a highly dysfunctional car manufacturing plant into a success.

The importance of underlying assumptions cannot be underestimated. Edgar Schein, a world-renowned expert on organizational culture, describes underlying assumptions as the source of values—and eventually behaviors and actions for defining culture—in his 2010 book, *Organization Culture and Leadership*. This means if you have Theory Y or positive assumptions about the potential of people, then you are well positioned to build trust with people on your team. This is important, because building trust inside your team is vital; without it, collaboration is all but impossible.

Many of the reasons managers struggle to manage their teams are related to their underlying assumptions. For example, a manager with Theory X assumptions—who does not trust people on their team—often has difficulty delegating. By looking closer at their underlying assumptions, managers can try to determine why they hold them and their source. (Use the Theory X—Theory Y tool in the appendix to judge your preferences.)

Lead With Mindset

The process for learning a new mindset starts with understanding the operating principles discussed in the "Mindset and Skill Set" section. Once you've internalized them, you'll have a foundation in place to leverage them with your team. You should use every opportunity to articulate the operating principles as often as needed through repetition and modeling to help build your competence and commitment—and your team's understanding for how they are used for genuine collaborative teamwork.

It is important to understand that the "whole is greater than the sum of the parts." Synergies generated by leading with a mindset for practicing genuine collaborative leadership will produce highly productive teams. Without that recognition—and application—the opportunity to find win-win solutions to the challenges your team encounters will be limited.

Your ability to consistently apply the operating principles will dictate if the team believes you're a manager with a collaborative mindset. Walking the talk here is all about being mindful of the tradeoffs involved in making decisions.

Develop Skill Set

Once you've internalized the operating principles, the next step involves the competencies focused on collaboration skills. By developing the competencies aligned with each operating principle, you'll start to acquire a deeper understanding and appreciation of the mindset needed to fully support practicing genuine team collaboration. I like to describe this as a never-ending cycle where the collaboration mindset not only helps shape or frame an individual's (and team's) application of the collaboration competencies, but also serves to motivate their interest or desire to acquire the needed competence. (See the Collaboration Operating Platform tool in the appendix for a detailed description of each competency.)

The process for developing collaboration competencies is highly personalized. Here, your development should include learning what each competency is, as well as how it's used and developed.

Bruce Griffiths (2015), a thought leader in competency development, uses an iceberg to describe the visible and hidden parts of a competency, with the "pattern of behavior associated with effective performance" sitting above the surface, and assumptions, values, thoughts and feelings, and personality lying below the surface (Figure 3-4).

Once you're comfortable with the language, the development process moves on to diagnosis. One option that's relatively easy to administer is to have your supervisor or people on your team rank which competencies are essential for your role. Bruce Griffiths describes this as a card-sort exercise, where competencies from the inventory are sorted into three categories: exceptional, proficient, and needs development. Another development option is to schedule a 360-degree survey, which captures feedback from your supervisor, peers, and direct reports. A third option is to target a small number of competencies essential for exceptional performance in your role as a frontline manager.

Figure 3-4. Visible and Hidden Competency Components

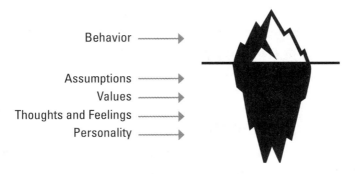

Behavior ⟶

Assumptions ⟶
Values ⟶
Thoughts and Feelings ⟶
Personality ⟶

Regardless of which option you use to identify knowledge or performance gaps, your ability to successfully apply the collaboration competencies is tied to being mindful of which competencies are aligned with each collaboration operating principle.

Delegate to Collaborate

When it comes to your effectiveness as the team's manager, it's important to understand that management is an influence process. This is even more critical for managing people on teams that succeed by applying a collaborative mindset.

You will be required to use multiple styles to manage people and your team. However, delegation is a key style for practicing genuine team collaboration. For example, if you believe that innovation is driven by team members having the competence and commitment to generate ideas for producing solutions in real time, then you must delegate to be effective. The key qualifier here is both the individual's and the team's commitment to apply the collaboration mindset, coupled with their competence to apply the collaboration competencies. Anything short of that and you may not be able to apply a delegating style.

Applying a service orientation for meeting your people's needs over time will allow you to adjust your style to meet the individual's or the team's needs. This takes willingness and competence on your part. Unfortunately, most managers are unable to effectively use more than one style, so the idea that you can develop and use multiple styles can be very intimidating. Yet, this skill set is critical to being perceived as a manager who is responsive to meeting the needs of your people and the team. For example, if an individual or team struggles on a project after you've delegated the assignment, you will likely need to use a different leadership style to get them back on track.

Build a Culture of Collaboration

Nurturing a team culture that encourages collaboration is critical to your team's success. Research shows that without a team culture firmly in place, your team will struggle. Strategies for developing a culture of collaboration for your team may include using Gallup's Q-12 as part of your game plan.

In 1998, the Gallup organization identified the 12 worker beliefs that had the biggest role in triggering a profitable, productive workplace. Their study was labeled the *Q-12,* based on 12 questions and their direct relationship to the bottom line, such as profits and productivity. Authors Marcus Buckingham and Curt Coffman described the Q-12 in *First Break All the Rules* (1999) as the simplest and most accurate way to measure the strength of a workplace. (For more information about the 12 questions, see chapter 4.)

Using mountain climbing as a metaphor to describe the order for managing the questions—that is, base camp, camp one, camp two, and camp three—you, as team manager, must focus initially on the two questions that are listed in Base Camp, followed next by the four questions listed under Camp One. These are the most powerful questions for developing a positive culture. Once you've addressed these six questions, you are well positioned to deal next with questions under Camp Two and finally those under Camp Three (Figure 3-5).

Figure 3-5. Q-12 Questions and Their Respective Camps

Question	Level
12. This last year, have I had the opportunities to learn and grow?	Camp Three
11. In the last six months, has someone at work talked to me about my progress?	Camp Three
10. Do I have a best friend at work?	Camp Two
9. Are my co-workers committed to doing quality work?	Camp Two
8. Does the mission of my company make me feel that my job is important?	Camp Two
7. At work, do my opinions seem to count?	Camp Two
6. Is there someone at work who encourages my development?	Camp One
5. Does my supervisor, or someone at work, seem to care about me as a person?	Camp One
4. In the last seven days, have I received recognition or praise for doing good work?	Camp One
3. At work, do I have the opportunity to do what I do best every day?	Camp One
2. Do I have the materials and equipment I need to do my work right?	Base Camp
1. Do I know what is expected of me at work?	Base Camp

A second key finding from the study that syncs up with my experience managing as well as working with managers was the discovery that the manager—not pay, benefits, perks, or a charismatic corporate leader—was the critical factor in building a strong workplace. Obviously, this is significant; it supports the idea that people join organizations and leave due to their managers' ineffectiveness.

When I served as vice president of HR in my last job, we used the Q-12 because it matched our definition of a positive work environment for motivating employees. The message to our frontline managers was centered on asking them to manage those things we could control, described in the first six questions, versus trying to deal with each employee on a one-to-one level when it came to motivation. Employees who were motivated to respond in a positive way to the working environment we created ended up being highly productive. Those who did not ended up being redirected and coached before being dismissed, if necessary.

<><><><><><><><><><><><><><><><><><><><><><><><><><><><><><><><><><><><><><><><><><>

Creating a Culture of Safety

When I served as vice president of HR for a midsize, publicly traded manufacturing company, we used the Q-12 as a key part of our organization development infrastructure to help track employee engagement levels, determine training needs, and manage culture change. The company I worked for manufactured a product that was big and dangerous to work around, and when we started the culture change effort we had a poor safety record with a very high OSHA Incident Rate. Obviously, the board of directors was concerned and asked us to respond.

The Q-12 was part of our change strategy to help create a safety culture. Over time (1998-2013), by applying the Q-12 to each of our nine business units, we were able to reduce our OSHA Incident Rate from 11.3 to 3.2. This brought us well below the industry benchmark and a reduction of 71 percent! We focused on Base Camp and Camp One initiatives, targeting our frontline managers and employees who were working on the floor in areas with high exposure to the products being manufactured. This also included focusing our leadership training efforts on frontline managers to equip them with the skill set to support a new culture.

Interestingly, in creating a culture of safety, we had to move away from Theory X assumptions to Theory Y assumptions. This shift addressed the need to move away from a compliance mindset to commitment mindset. Here, we believed that commitment trumped compliance when it came to safety management. That is, committed employees were internally motivated to manage their safety, as compared with forcing employees to be safe under the "comply or else" threat. We were able to shift the culture from a state of dependence to a state of independence. Finally, we shifted to a state of interdependence, where our frontline managers effectively modeled leadership and influenced highly engaged workers.

In this instance, the essential operating principles I applied to make the culture shift were develop partners on the field, rely on one another, and charge the team to perform the work.

Apply Collaboration's Operating Platform

Let's explore how the collaboration operating platform might play out in a hypothetical case.

Say you are a manager of a team working on a project and are asked to resolve issues brought up by a key stakeholder who also happens to be a long-term client. Your client has proposed a change to a project that is already a third complete. While the proposed change has merit, it would also expand the project's scope beyond the original parameters, which could delay the project's completion date and exceed budget projections. As a result, you're faced with the question: How can you integrate the client's proposed change in the project?

Your decision will reveal two important things: your assumptions or beliefs about the situation (your mindset) and your competence or ability to act in the situation (your skill set).

If you who work with any kind of customer—internal or external—on a project basis, you'll recognize the key phrase, "Wouldn't it be great if . . . " This is a sure sign that the project scope is going to be challenged—a change introduced at this point is going to delay the project.

So, you're faced with two options: Hold a team meeting to decide how to proceed or simply tell the client that the team will deliver on their request. On the one hand, the first option is a more inclusive choice, inviting the team's input for solving the problem, but it may be riskier if time is a concern. On the other hand, the second option puts the client first, at the risk of upsetting the team, and it puts the project's key performance indicators at risk: schedule, budget, and quality.

If you made the first choice, you promoted the operating principle, coach teams to respond to changing conditions on their own, demonstrating a collaborative mindset. Note that while there are other operating principles in play in this scenario, this was the key or leading principle. However, if you made the second choice, you did not demonstrate a collaborative mindset.

In this hypothetical case, the aforementioned collaboration operating principle helped shape or frame the team's decision to hold a team meeting, applying four collaboration competencies aligned with this principle. The first is team management, which aligns strictly to your role as the manager. The other three relate to shared competencies applied within the team: change agility, problem solving and decision making, and communicativeness.

The team's purpose for collaborating is to drive creative, real-time problem solving and entertain the possibility of changing direction. This also requires communication. The team's ability to be successful is directly related to both their commitment to develop competence in the competencies used herein and their commitment to apply these competencies. At the end of the day, each team member should ask if their effort contributed to the team's work, and if they were consistent with the team's norms.

Figure 3-6 lists the key behaviors for each of the three shared team competencies, described as patterns of behavior associated with each competency. Again, each team member's competence determines how successful the team performs in managing its customer's request. Is the team able to act in a way that is consistent with the essential operating principle identified in this case for practicing team collaboration?

A question that often comes up in debriefing this case deals with managing team conflict: Would the team be successful if conflict surfaced in their decision-making process? The answer deals with understanding that these three essential competencies may not be the only ones that come into play in this or any other case. For example, the conflict management competency could be applied, if needed. Although it's not described as an essential competency, it would become valuable if conflict surfaced as part of the team's decision-making process.

Figure 3-6. Mapping Example: Operating Principles, Essential Competencies, and Patterns of Behaviors

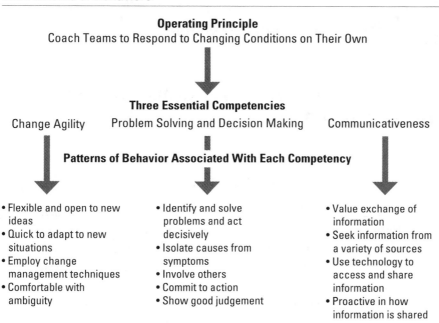

Operating Principle
Coach Teams to Respond to Changing Conditions on Their Own

Three Essential Competencies

Change Agility   Problem Solving and Decision Making   Communicativeness

Patterns of Behavior Associated With Each Competency

- Flexible and open to new ideas
- Quick to adapt to new situations
- Employ change management techniques
- Comfortable with ambiguity

- Identify and solve problems and act decisively
- Isolate causes from symptoms
- Involve others
- Commit to action
- Show good judgement

- Value exchange of information
- Seek information from a variety of sources
- Use technology to access and share information
- Proactive in how information is shared

This example shows how competencies may overlap and build on one another depending on the situation. It also reinforces the need to have multiple competencies available (and developed) in the team's inventory for the team to be effective. When combined, the three essential competencies applied in this case provide the best opportunity for the team to target behaviors for solving the client's request, which demonstrates genuine team collaboration.

Figure 3-7 gives a quick snapshot of how you combine underlying assumptions, operating principles, and competencies to achieve an outstanding team.

Figure 3-7. Collaboration Operating Platform

Collaboration Mindset		Collaboration Skill Set	Outcome
Theory Y Assumptions	+ Operating Principles	+ Collaboration Competencies	= Outstanding Team Results

Collaboration Operating Platform: Lead With Mindset

What Makes a Winning Collaborative Team Coach?

◇◇

Laws of Attraction

Struggling to fully understand her new role as team coach, Robin walked back to her office wondering how her team would respond to the announcement. The change was part of the company's strategy, which called for using coaches in all departments to develop a coaching culture and help retain and accelerate talent development.

As manager of the company's financial services group, Robin felt like she had a good relationship with everyone on her team. There had been no turnover for three years and performance problems were limited to a few minor issues that had been addressed. The fact that her status on the team was expanding was not a concern because the company was providing coaching training. But it did feel a little redundant in a strange way.

Robin's mentor in her last company had been a great resource. He was a senior-level manager who shared his thinking with her on a regular basis. He was also one of the most intriguing people she ever met. His ability to pass along leadership lessons on a regular basis, for example, was both educational and entertaining. One lesson she recalled that may be relevant to her current situation was the idea that opposites co-exist in management, and that no two things are as closely related as opposites. The fact that she was going to both manage and coach appeared to be a real example. While she wasn't totally sure this equated to a profound truth, like "less is more," she was willing to go with it for now.

Perhaps managing and coaching were related, she concluded, as she left her office to meet her team. If that was the case, then her transition to team coach might even be seamless.

From Team Manager to Team Coach

Coaching increases employee engagement, improves productivity, and accelerates the achievement of results for both individuals and teams. Most of your coaching will focus on performance development, such as encouraging your team members to develop self-confidence, resourcefulness, and a belief in the value of their own decision making and skills, all of which are critical to collaboration.

Your ability to quickly shift roles and step into a coaching role requires a change in your skill set. For example, lecturing versus listening, controlling versus influencing, and valuing likeness versus valuing differences are a few of the important skills shifts or changes you'll have to make.

Serving as a team coach requires you to focus most of your attention on the individuals in your team. This will give you a better chance of encouraging people to take personal responsibility (and accountability) for their actions. While it's also true that you will need to work on the team, that by itself will not produce shared responsibility and accountability. Two important examples of this include managing the team's charter and managing team building. The former task is described in more detail in the next section of this chapter. The latter task, briefly reviewed here, deals with managing the changing nature of your team. Because teams are constantly in flux, your task will be to monitor its performance and adjust how you manage the team to keep them focused. You will find that your team's progression will likely go through four identifiable stages of performance on a given task: forming, storming, norming, and performing. Your ability to use multiple managing styles to support your team's needs is critical to your team's success. Again, if your team was struggling with the task at hand, a delegating approach would not make sense. Most likely, you would use an approach that required more help from you or from resources you were able to bring in to help the team get back on track.

It's also important to acknowledge that while coaching has many applications, we'll be focusing only on the key applications that sync up with material covered in this chapter.

Coach to Develop a Culture of Collaboration

The importance of culture cannot be overstated when it comes to collaboration. We know that technology continues to become an enabler of collaboration. However, if we believe that culture is a pattern of basic assumptions that were invented, discovered, or developed by a given group as it learns to cope with its problems, as described by Edgar Schein, then we must acknowledge that culture is critical to collaboration. That is, collaboration would never happen if we relied solely on technology.

Your road map for coaching calls for focusing on the components illustrated in Figure 3-8, the Team Mini Charter for Developing a Culture of Collaboration.

Figure 3-8. Team Mini Charter for Developing a Culture of Collaboration

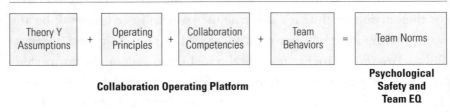

Typically, a team charter is described as a set of agreements that clearly describe what the team wants to accomplish, why it's important, and how the team will work together to achieve results. Most team charters have components that describe the team's vision, mission, purpose, values, norms, team member roles, key responsibility areas, team goals, communication strategies, decision-making authority and accountability, and available resources. I've limited this discussion on team charters to the components that are critical to practicing team collaboration. This means that your team remains responsible for addressing missing components in their team charter, such as team mission, once the team has been established.

Indeed, developing collaboration's team charter represents only a key piece of the larger operating framework for developing a culture of collaboration. Other components include HR systems and processes, compensation and rewards, and goal setting. Establishing a collaborative mindset at the top of the organization and cascading it down through the organization would be the most significant part of the framework.

Coach to Develop Collaboration's Team Mindset

You're charged with the task of creating a collaborative culture inside your work team. People on your team need to be coached on the collaboration mindset to fully leverage the team's time and energy.

Once this understanding is firmly in place, the next assignment is to introduce the operating principles. The key is to convince the team to embed these principles in the team's charter. You should spend adequate time exploring, shaping, and agreeing on a charter your team takes ownership in, both individually and a collectively. This may be your key coaching challenge and one that requires a commitment to provide ongoing coaching.

If your team is described as an intact team working on multiple tasks, high performance may not be needed for each task the team is working on. In that case, members of the team may function in a way that does not recognize the interdependent nature of their relationship. This means that collaboration should not be your team's default for all tasks; instead, its application is task specific. As the team's manager, this is a management application you will have to address, when necessary. For project teams, high performance is the likely operational mode your team will take on to accomplish the task.

Combating the Silo Mindset

Everyone knows that eliminating silos is key to both team and organizational success. Or do they? Why do silos continue to survive, and even thrive, in some organizations? In the age of collaboration, operating with silos is not good. Yet, they still exist and dominate an organization's culture. Teams who struggle with the silo mindset are going to be limited in how much real collaboration they experience.

I view the silo mindset as a fixed mindset and the collaboration mindset as a growth mindset. This conclusion is based on Stanford University Professor Carol Dweck's 2008 book, *Mindset: The New Psychology of Success,* in which she makes the distinction between a fixed mindset and a growth mindset, showing how mindset affects the way people live their lives. For example, people with a growth mindset possess the kind of perseverance and resilience they need to achieve creative solutions. This syncs up well to people who operate with a collaboration mindset.

Your coaching support should also include dealing with people who have underlying assumptions that support group work. In this case, your coaching should start with building your team's understanding that high performance is needed for the task at hand and can be achieved only when the team functions in a way that recognizes the interdependent nature of the team's relationship. Anything short of that recognition would not result in high performance.

Coach to Develop Collaboration's Team Skill Set

If you are not familiar with leadership development and coaching methodologies, the idea of teaching people a new range of competencies that focus on collaboration may seem like a challenging task. Developing team competence takes time, but it is not as complicated as you may think. Development options may include getting help from internal or external resources, including coaches.

With that said, the process for developing collaboration's competencies becomes highly personalized once people have been introduced to the competencies in this inventory. Again, the first step in your team's development may include explaining what competencies are and how they're used and developed.

You'll create an action plan once your team's strengths have been assessed across this inventory. Described as diagnosis, this first step can be done doing a card-sort exercise or by using a 360-degree survey instrument. From there, it's a case of targeting selected competencies for growth, and following that up with periodic coaching to help reinforce learning and application.

Coach to Develop Collaboration Team Norms

Developing team norms is the third area where coaching will be beneficial. Because norms are established by teams and used as ground rules for creating habits, your coaching should be centered on ensuring that your team's norms are improving team effectiveness.

Meaningful team norms typically address how the team makes decisions, how goals are managed, and how the team promotes shared responsibility and accountability. Team decision-making deals with building consensus and managing conflict. Goal setting addresses the need to manage shared agendas. And, gaining commitments across the team deals with modeling what you expect from others. These applications call for you to demonstrate inclusion in your actions as team coach. Without inclusiveness, there is no opportunity to tap into the talent on your team.

Because decision making is such a critical team norm, let's review a few key thoughts. First, the team's decision-making process will evoke a few emotions at times, prompting the need to manage conflict in a productive way. That's not always bad news, so long as the team's norm for managing conflict has been established, and conflict is treated as healthy so people on the team feel free to actively engage differences of opinion. Second, most new managers are not well equipped to manage conflict. I believe it is a specialized skill that calls for a commitment to develop conflict management skills as quickly as possible, so new managers need to jump in and get some training.

Talking about team conflict is a perfect segue to remind you that psychological safety is another key team norm for developing and managing a culture of collaboration. This means, for example, that your coaching must be proactive, and people need to see your coaching presence to ensure high performance.

It's also important to recognize that collaboration's operating platform has three essential conditions embedded into this framework to support psychological safety leading to high performance, as described by Jacqueline Peters and Catherine Carr (2013) in their research: clear boundaries; a sense of meaning, urgency, and impact; and team competence. The first two conditions are addressed in the collaboration operating principles, and the third is covered by the collaboration competencies.

Peters and Carr also describe three enabling conditions for supporting high performance in their research. First, does the team have a team charter that describes roles and responsibilities? Second, does the team work in an organization with a supportive infrastructure that provides adequate resources? And third, is team coaching established as part of the organization's platform to support the team's efforts, including using competent team coaches?

It's clear that "how" trumps "who" when it comes to team performance. That is, how people on the team work together is more important than who is on the team. When people are free to express themselves and take risks without feeling insecure or embarrassed, they have increased psychological safety. The collaboration operating platform provides a common framework and language for people on teams to expedite and optimize performance.

Coach to Develop Collaboration's Team EQ

Earlier in this chapter, I mentioned that managers who don't succeed typically lack self-awareness. The same can be said for teams. Teams that don't succeed typically lack self-awareness or team EQ.

By now you know that your team's EQ is very important for team effectiveness. Hopefully, you also recognize that it's actually a derivative of doing many things right, as we've discussed earlier in this chapter. For example, you know how important fostering trust and relationship building is to team success. You also know the importance of your team's charter, including how positive underlying assumptions support the application of the collaboration operating principles and competencies, eventually becoming habits for practicing genuine collaborative teamwork.

So, coaching calls for a personal commitment to continue building your team's self-awareness as you collaborate to achieve results. Use the framework described in this chapter to help build and maintain psychological safety inside your team. This includes targeting selected competencies from the inventory provided in the team's operating platform or in the EQ Model.

Conclusion

This chapter presented a new methodology or operating platform for developing managers (and people on teams) who can effectively practice genuine team collaboration on the job. Your task is to lead with a collaborative mindset and manage using the collaboration competencies to make you and your team better collaborators.

This methodology positions team coaching as a critical application to build and maintain your competence and commitment to practice team collaboration, leading to win-win outcomes. Not only will this make you a better collaborator, it will make you a better developer of talent.

As team manager, developing a culture of collaboration (on your team) is your highest priority. Without this in place, your efforts to produce winning outcomes will likely fall flat. This is the primary reason why collaboration fails to work in teams (and organizations).

Depending on your team's assignment, becoming more innovative may be its only real opportunity to demonstrate value creation. This task can be highly visible inside your organization because of its consequences to business growth and success. Your team must apply the collaboration operating platform inside a culture of collaboration.

Your learning journey is a never-ending challenge that requires personal commitment. Managers who succeed understand the importance of developing their self-awareness and commitment to continuous development and improvement.

4

Engagement

<<<<<<<<<<<<<<<<<<<<<<<<<<<<<<<<<<<<<<<<<<<<<<<<<<<<<<<<<<<<<<<<<<<<<<<<<<<<<<<<

Hunter Haines

Few topics have gained as much attention in organizations in the past 20 years as employee engagement. Why is that? In their efforts to seek out greater efficiency and productivity from their workforces, organizations have turned to determining which factors influence their overall success and that of their workers. As a result, they've uncovered the significant impact engaged employees have on organizational success. But how much impact? The Gallup organization, which has measured employee engagement for decades, reports that workplaces with the most engaged employees benefit from higher levels of productivity, improved quality, fewer safety incidents, increased customer loyalty, and higher sales and profitability, all while experiencing lower levels of absenteeism and employee turnover. In fact, almost every metric that's important to organizations can be positively affected by increases in employee engagement.

The good news for organizations is that engaging employees isn't rocket science. It doesn't require high-priced consultants or expensive training programs. It does require a recognition that employees have a choice about the amount of effort they expend in support of the organization's goals, and a willingness to create an environment where employees are inspired and motivated to be the best they can be. Increasingly, organizations are turning to their managers to create this engaging work environment.

I've been fascinated by the influence managers have on employee performance for as long as I can remember. My first full-time job was working as a receptionist in a doctor's office, which involved sitting at a desk behind a sliding glass window and greeting patients as they arrived. I had a bright, friendly, outgoing personality that I used to help our typically anxious patients feel more at ease. I was always at my desk when the office manager, Sharon, arrived. Each morning, the same ritual would occur:

"Good morning, Sharon," I would say, greeting her with a big smile as she walked through the waiting room. She would glance my way and then continue walking to her office without responding.

That morning ritual completely baffled me. I may have been new to the workforce but I was fairly certain that managers were supposed to help their employees, not squash their self-esteem! I don't know why Sharon refused to return my daily greeting, but it's likely she wasn't aware of the negative impact her behavior had on me, or her missed opportunity to reinforce my positive behaviors or highlight how my contributions benefited the business. Doing so would have helped me feel engaged in my work and eager to contribute.

These interactions with Sharon also became part of the inspiration for my career choice in talent development. Over the past 20 years, I've used this role to work with organizational leaders at all levels to understand the impact of their behavior on employee performance and to help employees perform at their best in support of the organization's goals. During this time, research on organizational performance has helped us understand more about how employee engagement drives employee performance.

In this chapter, we'll explore the impact managers can have on employees as we define employee engagement, identify factors that increase employee engagement, and pinpoint where managers should focus their efforts if they want to significantly increase employee engagement.

What Is Employee Engagement?

I often get asked whether *employee engagement* is just a new buzzword for employee satisfaction, which organizations have been measuring for decades. The answer is no—employee satisfaction and employee engagement are not the same. When organizations measure employee satisfaction, they are measuring how happy or content their employees are with the organization and with factors that affect their work, such as managers, pay, work environment, and so on. On the other hand, when organizations measure employee engagement, they're measuring how emotionally committed an employee is to the organization, and how willing they are to go above and beyond in support of the organization's goals. In other words, satisfaction is a measure of how an employee feels. Engagement is a measure of what an employee is likely to do—the amount of effort they will choose to devote to their work. It's the discretionary effort that engaged employees choose to exert that results in increased organizational performance. Engaged employees care about the success of their organizations and actually expend extra effort to help the organizations achieve their goals.

When I teach managers about employee engagement, I ask them to think of a time they were engaged at work and to describe what it felt like. I typically get the following responses:

- I enjoyed my work.
- I liked being there.
- I knew what I was supposed to do.
- I wanted to help my company be successful.
- It was important to me.
- It didn't feel like work.
- My work was meaningful.
- I knew I was making a difference.
- Time went by quickly.
- I felt supported by my manager.

The managers describe being engaged at work as a time when they enjoyed their work, understood their specific role, found meaning in their work, and knew how their work positively affected their organization. How does this compare with how the experts define employee engagement? Gallup (2018) defines engaged employees as "those who are involved in, enthusiastic about, and committed to their work and to their workplace." The Society for Human Resource Management (SHRM; 2017) describes employee engagement as "the connection and commitment employees exhibit toward an organization, leading to higher levels of productive work behaviors." In a nutshell, engaged employees find meaning and value in their work and are inspired to work hard to achieve organizational goals.

While most discussions about employee engagement focus on how it benefits the organization, the equation is not one-sided. Early research on employee engagement emphasized the benefits that employees receive when they are engaged. William Kahn (1990) defined personal engagement as "the simultaneous employment and expression of a person's 'preferred self' in task behaviors that promote connections to work and to others, personal presence, and active full role performances." In other words, engaged employees receive some level of personal return on investment for doing their jobs and are therefore driven to achieve what have become mutual goals. It is this mindset of *mutual benefit* that is at the heart of employee engagement.

What Creates Employee Engagement?

Researchers have worked over the past few decades to identify the factors that determine employee engagement. With new techniques and tactics flooding workplaces to boost engagement, it helps to start by running through how its influencers have come to light.

Early research on the topic looked at the factors that affect an employee's decision to complete tasks at work. Kahn (1990) identified three psychological conditions: meaningfulness, safety, and availability (Figure 4-1). According to Kahn, employees continually assess the extent to which these three psychological conditions are met as they decide how much effort to put into completing their work tasks.

Figure 4-1. Psychological Conditions That Influence Engagement

Dimension	Definition
Meaningfulness *(How meaningful is it to bring myself into this performance?)*	Sense of return on investment of self in role performances.
Safety *(How safe is it to do so?)*	Sense of being able to show and employ self without fear of negative consequences to self-image, status, or career.
Availability *(How available am I to do so?)*	Sense of possessing the physical, emotional, and psychological resources necessary for investing self in role performances.

In other words, when deciding how much effort to exert on a specific work task, employees continually assess: What's in it for me? Is there a potential negative consequence for completing the task? And am I physically and emotionally able to complete the task?

While Kahn's research provided a lens into how employees make task-related decisions, other research has focused on identifying specific factors that positively influence an employee's level of engagement at work. A Conference Board study identified 29 different factors of engagement measured by various researchers in the literature (Gibbons 2006). Of those factors, eight were identified by numerous researchers:

- trust and integrity of the management team
- nature of the job or work
- line-of-sight of the effect of contributions on company performance
- career growth opportunities
- overall pride in the company
- relationship with co-workers or team
- employee development opportunities
- relationship with immediate manager.

Other research studies found that three additional factors were important to engagement: employee recognition, pay fairness, and the amount of personal influence an employee possesses (Robinson, Perryman, and

Hayday 2004; Swindall 2007; Towers Perrin 2003).

Most notably, Gallup researchers spent decades studying factors that affect employee engagement before identifying 12 core elements that they believed were linked to business outcomes and workgroup performance. These elements, known as the Q12 Index, make up the 12 questions in their employee engagement survey:

1. Do you know what is expected of you at work?
2. Do you have the materials and equipment to do your work right?
3. At work, do you have the opportunity to do what you do best every day?
4. In the last seven days, have you received recognition or praise for doing good work?
5. Does your supervisor, or someone at work, seem to care about you as a person?
6. Is there someone at work who encourages your development?
7. At work, do your opinions seem to count?
8. Does the mission and purpose of your company make you think your job is important?
9. Are your associates (fellow employees) committed to doing quality work?
10. Do you have a best friend at work?
11. In the last six months, has someone at work talked to you about your progress?
12. In the last year, have you had opportunities to learn and grow?

Organizations are hoping an increased focus on employee engagement will not only help retain employees, but also attract new employees. To ensure employees have an employer worth committing to, organizations are rethinking their employee value propositions and paying attention to how their employees connect with the organization. The "Employee Experience," which is a concept that evolved from the "Customer Experience," encompasses all the ways potential, current, or former employees interact with an organization. Airbnb (2015) transformed its human resources department into the department of employee experience to "drive the company's health and happiness" and attract and retain the best and brightest employees. This department oversees all aspects of the employee's experience, from food service to technology to office space.

Organizations such as Airbnb realize that employee engagement is not just the right thing to do, but a strategic necessity to attract and retain a high-performing workforce. From new employee orientation to employee training and retiree benefits, employees want to know that the organization is committed to their success. Increasing employee engagement requires the organization to recognize that employees have a choice about the amount of effort they expend in support of its goals and to be willing to create a work environment where employees can be engaged.

Not all engagement factors are completely within the manager's or organization's control, however, and some may not be under their control at all. There are many factors that affect an employee's ability to bring their full selves to work in support of their goals and the goals of the organization. Some people are intrinsically motivated by the work they do, while others may be more motivated by factors outside work, such as hobbies, church, or volunteering. For others, life circumstances such as physical or emotional health, finances, or family responsibilities can influence their ability to be engaged. An employee who is nearing retirement may be more focused on starting their new life chapter than finding meaning at work. A new parent may find it difficult just to stay awake!

To have the greatest impact on employee engagement, organizations should focus on factors they can influence. And more and more, they're discovering that those factors are the manager's responsibility. Gallup (2015) estimates that as much as 70 percent of the variance in employee engagement across business units is attributable to managers. I have seen this in person while teaching and coaching thousands of managers and employees over the past 20 years. When leaders actively seek to motivate, inspire, and support employees, the result is a work environment where employees can be engaged. Leadership effectiveness at all levels is something organizations can, and should, optimize to enhance employee engagement.

Why Don't Managers Engage Employees?

Most managers believe they're good at managing people. Of the thousands I've worked with, very few believed they needed to improve their ability to lead people. On the other hand, I've also met with thousands of employees who believe their managers could do a better job of helping them perform! Why the disconnect? There are several reasons.

People are often promoted to management roles as a way for organizations to retain them. This is because, in most organizations, the only way to significantly increase an employee's salary is to move them into a management role where pay scales are typically higher and bonuses are often provided. Very few organizations have compensation structures that allow them to pay individual contributors at the same rate as those in a management position. Unfortunately, using management positions as a retention strategy is a recipe for creating managers who don't really want to manage people and lack the skills to do so effectively.

In addition, many managers are promoted into their roles because of their knowledge and success with the technical aspects of their jobs. I've worked with managers who were brilliant in their areas of expertise (such as medicine, engineering, plumbing, sales, and so on), but had no idea how to get the best performance from people because they had never been taught how to do it. Even worse, they often weren't held accountable for their "people-leading" responsibilities. Their departments might have low performance or significant employee turnover, but as long as they continue to contribute to the organization, these individual-contributors-turned-managers are left alone to do their damage. Organizations that promote technical experts into management roles often lose their best individual contributors and gain ineffective managers.

Thus, most managers are "working managers." In addition to managing people, they're also responsible for contributing in some way to the work that is produced by their departments. This can result in managers feeling overwhelmed. They not only forget that their primary role is to help employees be successful, but also fail to demonstrate that their primary role is to help employees be successful. Every manager I've ever asked knows their employees watch everything they do. Employees are looking for management behaviors and listening for words that reinforce their belief about whether their manager is truly committed to helping them be successful. In other words, they want to know that their manager is credible.

As mentioned previously, organizations don't always make the effort to identify the skills managers need to be effective. They often spend considerable time and effort developing complex career ladders for critical positions such as nurses and financial analysts, but they do a poor job of defining, identifying, and implementing competencies for managers. Of the organizations in the 2016 ATD ACCEL study, only 46 percent had identified key skills related to managerial success. Organizations need to ask, "What do our managers need to do to be successful?" "What do our managers need to know?" "How do our managers need to behave?"

Managers are not always held accountable for engaging employees and driving performance. I have been asked to coach managers who have derailed somehow in their roles, only to find out they've been failing for years and no one had done anything to support them or their employees. Why were they allowed to remain in their roles with such poor performance? When manager effectiveness is addressed, it's often coming from a reactive mindset rather than proactive one. Organizations address poor managerial performance after seeing a negative financial impact to the organization. Employee satisfaction and engagement surveys are used to identify managers that are not performing well, without having first established clear performance expectations or investing in development initiatives to help managers be successful.

These situations are far too common and result in missed opportunities to drive employee performance and engagement and contribute to organizational success. However, they offer an opportunity for organizations to refocus efforts on the critical role managers can have in inspiring and motivating employees and driving engagement.

The Essential Role of Managers in Driving Employee Engagement

The typical manager is responsible for establishing employee performance goals, monitoring performance and attendance, and providing performance feedback. In doing these tasks, managers can drive employee performance and engagement by demonstrating a commitment to the employee's success. Managers who take the time to create and sustain supportive relationships with employees, and intentionally connect with them about what's important to both the organization and to the employee, create environments that encourage employees to find meaning in their work, feel supported, and invest their full selves in support of the organization's goals. Ultimately, managers engage employees when they do six things: support, share, value, meet, coach, and involve.

1. Create and Sustain Supportive Relationships

While managers are responsible for motivating each employee to deliver their best performance, the specific motivators for each employee will differ. Learning what motivates each employee requires managers to build supportive relationships by getting to know their employees and consistently demonstrating their commitment to the employee's success. Getting to know an employee takes time, but there are ways a manager can speed it up.

As early as possible in the relationship, I encourage managers to let employees know that their job is to help employees be successful. It's often assumed that employees know this, but hearing it directly from their manager can reassure employees that they will be supported. To help them be successful at completing a task or working on a project, managers should proactively provide as much information and guidance as possible, and encourage employees to ask questions to clarify expectations and attain needed support. Positively responding to questions and requests for support will encourage employees to continue to ask questions and ask for help when needed.

Over time, managers will learn what type of support each employee typically needs to successfully complete tasks and assignments. Rather than wait, managers can ask employees what support they need when assigning a task or project. This is a more helpful approach than trying to guess what type of support an employee needs, which can result in a mismatch between the support needed and the support provided. Too little support can make an employee feel unimportant; too much support can cause the employee to feel distrusted. Being proactive can help build trust between managers and employees; trust that employees won't be perceived as incompetent if they need information or assistance and trust that they will be supported if they make a mistake. A supportive environment is a safe environment where employees can focus on achieving goals rather than protecting themselves from judgment and negative consequences.

Developing employees is a way to let them know you want them to be successful. To increase engagement, managers can ask about their employees' professional strengths and interests, and look for ways to use and develop these strengths and interests in their current positions. Initial opportunities for employee development should focus on the knowledge and skills employees need to be fully competent in their current role. When an employee is fully competent and confident in their current role, there may be an opportunity to focus on development to help an employee prepare for a lateral move or a promotion.

Committing to employee success includes knowing the employee's career goals and helping them take steps to achieve them. Managers should keep in mind that an employee's current job may not be their dream job and, as a result, they may not be as fulfilled or engaged as they could be. It took me years to figure out what I wanted to be when I grew up. During that time, I worked in many jobs that weren't exactly my dream job: In addition to my years as a medical receptionist, I scooped ice cream, walked dogs, taught computer skills, and trained employees on guidelines for government grants and contracts. As rewarding as these jobs may be for some, they didn't fulfill me and they didn't often motivate me to go above and beyond. What would have motivated me was a manager who knew that these jobs were simply stepping stones to a more fulfilling job and helped me figure out and attain my dream job.

Employee development has another benefit. Managers who aspire to move up in organizations should consider deepening their departmental bench strength. If managers aren't developing someone to move into their role, they may be overlooked when the organization is looking at succession planning. The most important step a manager can take to prepare for a promotion is to make sure there is a competent and confident successor available to move into their role.

2. Share Organizational Information

Driving engagement is all about helping employees find meaning in their work. What better way to help them find meaning than by regularly sharing and reinforcing the organization's purpose and vision. The alternative means keeping them in the dark, whether purposefully or accidentally, and depriving them of information that could help them do their jobs. When employees understand the organization's mission, its vision for the future, the key strategic goals, and how their jobs help achieve those goals, they are more likely to make decisions that are aligned with organizational goals.

Managers typically share relevant company information with employees when they're hired, but they often fail to share company news and events on an ongoing basis. Regularly connecting the work employees are doing with the organization's mission, vision, and goals is a way to help them see how their work positively affects the organization's success and find meaning in their work. Another key responsibility is translating the organization's strategic goals into meaningful work objectives and outcomes that will achieve the goals. Managers can help employees understand the importance of the organization's strategy and how each employee's contribution matters. With their knowledge of the actual work their direct reports are doing, managers are best equipped to share inspirational stories about how the organization's products or services make a difference to customers and then translate these stories to each individual direct report's contributions.

Managers typically attend organizational leadership meetings and are expected to cascade select information to their employees. Unfortunately, this doesn't always happen. When employees aren't kept informed, they can feel unimportant or disrespected. To avoid this, managers should share as much information as they can with their employees. There may be information that's not appropriate for a manager to share (such as an upcoming reorganization or other business strategy), but keeping them informed about key organizational initiatives helps employees feel valued and respected, builds trust, and helps create an environment where employees can be engaged.

3. Help Employees Feel Valued Through Frequent Feedback

If I could hang a huge banner in the front of every management class I've ever taught, it would read, "Everyone Wants to Be Valued and Respected." Employees perform best when this is true for them. Most employees come to work and want to contribute to the success of the organization. When as a manager you recognize the strengths they bring to the team, the effort they expend, and the contributions they make, it helps them know they're making a difference. And when they know they're making a difference, it helps them find meaning in their work, which affects their commitment to the organization and their willingness to go above and beyond. It helps keep them engaged.

When an employee doesn't feel valued and respected, it detracts from their ability to be engaged. Even worse, it can result in low performance and inappropriate behavior. When employees act out in the workplace, it's often not related to their work. It's more likely due to the person feeling undervalued or not respected. One manager I worked with was frustrated by an employee who had a bad attitude. She said the employee exerted just enough effort to complete a task and was defensive when given feedback for improvement. I asked the manager if the employee ever did anything well. She said, "Of course." I then asked about the last time she had given the employee positive feedback, and she couldn't remember.

Of course, managers shouldn't allow employees to have bad attitudes, but in my experience, if employees don't feel valued by their manager, they often have a bad attitude! Even if an employee is a low performer, they're likely doing something that adds value to the team. When they feel good about themselves and believe that you appreciate them, they're more likely to want to help the organization succeed.

I've coached many managers who tell me it's not their job to help employees feel better about themselves. These same managers often say they shouldn't have to give an employee praise for simply doing their jobs. Often, because these managers don't want or need a lot of positive feedback, they think that their employees don't need positive feedback either. In fact, they assign negative judgment to positive feedback. What they fail to recognize is that letting employees know they are valued has a huge impact on an employee's feelings of self-worth—if they want employees to perform at their best, they need to make sure their employees feel valued. Once these managers realize that they need to value and respect people because they will likely perform better—when they realize there is something in it for them—they get it. Essentially, you're reaffirming your commitment to the employee, which is essential if you want them to demonstrate commitment to you and the organization.

Every interaction with an employee is an opportunity for a manager to ensure the employee feels valued and respected. However, that doesn't mean managers need to lavish false praise every chance they get. They simply need to make sure employees feel good about themselves and are able to invest their best selves in their work. Similarly, treating employees with respect, as fully capable and competent adult human beings, tends to build mutual respect. Every communication a manager has with an employee, even if they're providing feedback for improvement, can and should be carried out in a way that is respectful. This includes understanding whether they want less positive feedback or more. People are different. It's the manager's responsibility to learn what each employee needs to perform at their best. If a manager has a span of control that makes this impossible (such as too many direct reports), consider whether this keeps them from providing the essential feedback that drives engagement and performance.

Positive feedback lets employees know whether they've achieved the desired result or are on the right track. The most effective positive feedback is specific. When managers are specific about what employees have done well when they give feedback, they'll know exactly what to do next time. What gets recognized gets repeated. While it may feel good to be told you've done "a good job," letting an employee know specifically what they've done well lets them know what to keep doing in the future.

Showing that you value and respect employees creates a trusting environment where they feel safe to contribute. According to Patrick Lencioni, a well-known management speaker and author of numerous management books including *The Five Dysfunctions of a Team* (2002), trust is the foundation of a high-performing team. Lencioni's concept of "vulnerability-based trust" refers to an environment where employees feel safe disagreeing with one another, asking for help, and admitting when they've made a mistake, without the fear of negative consequences. Disagreement, also known as constructive conflict, helps teams collaboratively achieve the best results for the group and the organization. In a safe environment, employees can disagree with their manager in a way that is respectful, focused on achieving the best results, and free of concerns about negative consequences.

To create vulnerability-based trust, Lencioni encourages team members to take the time to get to know one another. It is through self-disclosure (low levels of appropriate personal disclosure) that people learn one another's motives, intent, goals, values, and emotions—in other words, their humanity. When this happens, they often realize what they have in common and are more willing to contribute ideas and work toward shared goals.

One of my favorite activities to use with teams to help them get to know one another better and increase trust is to ask them to draw, without words, two things on chart paper:

- something they are proud of
- a life goal they have not yet achieved.

In one group I worked with, everyone shared how proud they were of their families. The recognition of this shared value improved trust and an increased willingness to share ideas and suggestions about how the team could succeed.

By letting employees know they are valued and interacting with them in a respectful manner on a regular basis, managers demonstrate their commitment to employee success.

4. Hold Regular One-on-One Meetings

To further demonstrate a commitment to employee success, managers should regularly meet with each employee so they can share what they are working on, what's going well, what's not going well, and ask for any needed support. The frequency and duration of these one-on-one meetings will depend on the number of direct reports a manager has, the type of work the employees do, and how often they need support.

I often hear from managers that they don't have enough time in their schedules to hold one-on-one meetings with each of their direct reports. This is particularly true in healthcare, where nurse managers can have upward of 100 direct reports. When managers can't regularly meet with staff one-on-one, they need to find a way to regularly connect with each of their direct reports, even if it's just a few minutes while walking down the hall, to ask if they need any support and follow up on any requests for support.

Best practices for one-on-one meetings include:

- Asking the employees to schedule the one-on-one meetings to build ownership.
- Allowing the employee to start the meeting and share what they are working on.
- Not canceling the meeting if it can be avoided. Canceling an employee's one-on-one meeting could send the message that the meeting is not important and, even worse, that they are not important.

As employees are sharing what they're working on, managers should ask what support they need. Then they can provide appropriate feedback and coaching to assist the employee. After the employee has covered their agenda, managers can use any remaining time to share key organizational information.

I'm always surprised by the number of managers who don't hold regular one-on-one meetings with their direct reports. While the primary purpose of these meetings is to provide an opportunity for employees to receive needed support, they also allow managers to keep their fingers on the pulse of the department by hearing from employees about what's going on. Managers can learn about opportunities to positively affect employee performance or behavior, or identify actions they may need to take to maintain a positive, respectful work environment.

Recently I had the opportunity to coach a busy nurse manager who was having trouble getting her staff to collaborate with one another. She encouraged them in monthly staff meetings to work together but was consistently hearing through the grapevine that certain employees weren't cooperating. When I asked, she said she had not been scheduling regular one-on-one meetings with her staff. We discussed how the one-on-one meetings would allow her to ask each staff member how the collaboration was going, and to coach them individually on how to navigate challenging interactions. When I checked back three months later, during which time she had been having consistent one-on-one meetings, she said she had given individualized coaching to each person to help reinforce expectations, as well as supported the individual development of each employee. She said staff members were soon collaborating more effectively in support of the department's goals.

When combined with regular team meetings, one-on-one meetings help managers provide employees with the direction, guidance, information, and support they need. When employees feel supported, they are more likely to be engaged in their work.

5. Use a Coaching Approach to Improve Performance

Once a manager has helped employees understand how their role adds value to the organization and clarified what is expected of them, it's time for managers to observe performance and provide feedback. Feedback is information about how employees are performing their work. It is unlikely employees will perform every task well on their first attempt. Providing feedback is an essential managerial role to help improve employee performance and thus increase engagement in their work.

In the bestselling book *The One Minute Manager,* authors Ken Blanchard and Spencer Johnson compare a lack of performance feedback to bowling with a curtain down over the pins. Without the ability to see the pins, a bowler has no way of knowing whether the ball knocked down any pins or which pins to aim for next. Performance feedback gives employees the information they need to do their jobs successfully. How managers provide feedback can have a significant impact on employee engagement and performance.

When I ask managers to tell me the most challenging aspect of managing people, I usually hear the same thing—personalities. They tell me that differences in personalities make it difficult to know how people will react to feedback. They share stories of giving feedback for improvement to employees who cried or got angry. One manager told me she was afraid the conversation would turn into a confrontation. To avoid a potential confrontation, managers often avoid giving any feedback at all. Not only is this unhelpful for the employee who needs the feedback, it often results in other employees feeling disrespected because their manager won't give their colleagues feedback they need to hear.

When managing people, the two areas that managers must always be focused on are performance and behavior. When performance drops or employees behave in a manner that is inappropriate in the workplace, managers must address it. The problem is, many managers lack the confidence and competence to effectively provide feedback for improvement in a way that will be heard and acted on. I often hear from people that their managers don't hold their peers accountable for performance or behavior.

Most of us don't like receiving feedback for improvement. The thought of getting "constructive feedback" instantly makes us anxious and uncomfortable. When not delivered well, feedback for improvement can feel like an attack, which causes our natural flight or fight response to kick in. We either get defensive (fight) or feel defeated (flight). It's hard to perform well when you don't feel good about yourself.

So how can managers provide feedback for improvement in a way that it's heard and acted on? By using a coaching approach. A coaching approach turns feedback for improvement into a conversation rather than a statement. It requires managers to connect with employees in a way that lets them know that what they do matters. It starts with the mindset that employees want to be successful, and sometimes need guidance and direction to do so. The role of the manager is to provide this to help them be successful.

Think of a time when someone in your life gave you feedback that made a difference to your success. Maybe it was feedback that was hard to hear. As a teenager, I attended a weekly youth group session at my church. After one session, Wendy, one of our youth group leaders, pulled me aside and said, "Hunter, you have many valuable contributions to our discussions, but it would be a lot easier to listen to you if you didn't use the word *like* so much." At first, I was embarrassed. Was I *really* hard to listen to? But then I began to pay attention to how much I used *like,* and I consciously stopped using it. I'm confident that Wendy helped me be a more effective communicator.

Wendy didn't have to give me that feedback; she did because she wanted me to be successful. What matters is caring enough about your employees to give them feedback. You may be the only one who cares enough about their success to take the time and effort to skillfully deliver a message in a way that is going to be heard and acted on. Taking this time to invest in an employee's development shows that you and the organization care.

The following guidelines can help managers use a coaching approach to give feedback for improvement in a way that actually results in improved performance:

- **Strategically give feedback for improvement.** Plan what you want to accomplish by giving the feedback. Think about how you want the employee to feel and how you want them to perform after you share the feedback. Don't give feedback for improvement "off the cuff"; choose your words carefully. Everything you say will be interpreted by the recipient in the context of their needs, hopes, and concerns. Be sure to say what you mean and check for their understanding. Avoid generalizations and emotionally charged words, such as *never, always,* and *should.* Instead, describe the specific behavior or actions taken, and try phrases and words such as *There are times when . . .* or *often* or *frequently.* Ask yourself questions such as:

> » How can I communicate this information so the person will be receptive?
> » What do I want to be improved?
> » What do I want to change?
> » What specific ideas or suggestions can I offer?

- **Clarify your motivation.** Before giving feedback for improvement, identify and evaluate your expectations of others. Are those expectations realistic, fair, appropriate, valid, pertinent, and necessary? Or are they just the way you want things done? What's in it for the person receiving the feedback? Feedback for improvement can help employees learn and develop skills. Make sure the feedback you give is intended to be helpful for the employee.

- **Share your good intent.** Usually, your intent is very good; you want the person to be more successful, you want them to develop new skills, and so on. However, we often forget to share our good intent, because we assume the other person knows it. If you don't share your intent, the other person will make it up and could assume your intent is not good.

- **Plan for the employee's possible reactions.** We all take feedback personally. Unfortunately, most of us have been on the receiving end of feedback for improvement that was not given well. As a result, when receiving feedback for improvement, we can experience a variety of reactions (surprise, shock, anger, defensiveness, rationalization, or acceptance). It's important to plan for these reactions, think through what the person's objections might be, and plan how to overcome them. Plan also for how you will manage your own emotions during the interaction.

- **Be empathetic.** Feedback for improvement can cause employees to become defensive and emotional. We all need to be heard and understood. Try to connect with how they are feeling, let them know you understand why they might feel that way, and then focus back on the expected performance or behavior.

- **Help protect the person's self-esteem.** Damaging a person's self-esteem will likely prevent them from hearing and acting on your feedback. Are there ways you can help them feel valued, even if you're giving them feedback for improvement? Phrases that can help with this include, "You're an important member of the team" and "We count on you for . . . " Give the employee the benefit of the doubt by saying, "You may not be aware of the impact of your behavior." Let them know you support them and have confidence in their ability to be successful.

- **Keep your feedback for improvement future focused.** Use phrases such as, "The next time you . . . "

- **Make sure the environment and timing is appropriate.** Choose a time when you and the other person are in the right frame of mind. A good rule of thumb is to never give feedback when you are angry. Be respectful and provide feedback for improvement in a private setting.

- **Use good questions to help employees consider alternatives.** Avoid "why" questions because they may cause the person to be defensive. Instead, use "how" and "what" questions such as, "How do you think you could do this differently next time?" or "What other ways could you try?"

While managers are expected to give feedback for improvement, it doesn't have to result in hurt feelings or defensive behavior. If approached from a coaching perspective, feedback for improvement can be given in a way that is respectful and effective. In fact, some managers are so effective at giving feedback that employees feel better about themselves after they receive it!

Providing effective feedback and coaching is another way for managers to demonstrate their commitment to employee success.

6. Involve Employees

Another way to drive engagement is to encourage employees to provide input and innovate, especially when it's used to positively affect the organization. To the extent possible, managers should involve employees when developing performance objectives and measures. This increases their commitment to the work because they'll start to own the process.

Of course, there might be times when a manager can't involve employees in developing their performance objectives. For example, the organization may have set quality or performance targets. In this case, managers can seek employees' input on how the work gets done by asking them, "What do we need to do as a team to meet these objectives?" As performance expectations change, initiate discussions with employees to provide guidance, allow them to ask questions, and make suggestions about the best way to meet the expectations. Telling employees what to do will likely result in compliance, whereas involving employees will likely result in commitment. When an employee is committed to their work, they're more likely to find meaning in it and invest themselves in achieving the goals. Organizations spend a lot of time sourcing, recruiting, interviewing, hiring, and orienting employees, but don't always utilize the strengths of the employee. They don't involve them or get their input. Instead, they use command and control leadership style, which can squash enthusiasm.

I once worked for a manager who was known for this style of management. I would have a great idea and excitedly head off to her office to share it. My co-workers, who knew this manager as well as I did, would literally try to stop me from going into her office, because they knew I would come out crushed. My boss needed to be right. No matter what idea I brought to her, she could always find a way to tell me why the idea wouldn't work. This behavior discouraged me from wanting to take any initiative; it was easier to just have her tell me what to do. This is not what my organization was paying me for. They had hired me for my skills and experience, and because of this manager, they were not getting it. I see this all the time in organizations, with managers shooting down their employees' ideas. The result? Employees stop sharing their ideas. At a time when companies are racing to come up with the next disruptive innovation, managers should encourage employees to generate and share ideas, not dismiss them.

Instead of shooting my ideas down, my former manager could have mentored me—helping explain why my ideas might not have worked in the organization. In their bestseller, *Love 'Em or Lose 'Em,* Beverly Kaye and Sharon Jordan-Evans use the acronym "Mentor" to define the role. A good mentor *models, encourages, nurtures,* and *teaches organizational reality.* Teaching organizational reality means helping employees avoid organizational minefields and be successful.

The Result

When asked to identify the barriers to exhibiting ACCEL skills, including engagement, managers indicated the top barrier was a lack of time, because other priorities continue to get in the way. In my experience, most managers think it will take too much time to do the right things. The opposite is true! Use the tips in the appendix to get started.

If you're like many of the managers I've worked with, you'll find that when you commit to helping employees be successful, it not only saves you time, it can make your job easier. When employees feel valued and respected, they stop comparing themselves with other employees. There is less drama. The workplace is more productive and respectful. You'll no longer avoid addressing employee behaviors and performance for fear that it will result in a confrontation. You'll find you can interact more effectively with individuals who have differing personalities and priorities. You'll be able to create a workplace culture where people feel respected, valued, and encouraged to be their best. If you do these things, your employees will thank you by achieving and exceeding your expectations and theirs.

5

Listening and Assessing

Michele Nevarez

I'm not always a great listener. In fact, most of us aren't as good at listening as we think we are.

Under stress, I am guilty of interrupting people, either to finish their sentence because I'm panicking about my limited time, or because I agree with what the person is saying and I'm anxious to share my affinity. I'm not trying to be rude. Sometimes what they're saying really resonates with my own view, and I'm simply excited to show my enthusiasm and agreement. But the impact of interrupting is damaging. As a manager, when I interrupt people, it's a direct message that I don't care what the other person has to say (even if that's not the case). The reason why I'm interrupting fails to matter.

In 2016, I became part of a start-up venture, and it's stressful. Unfortunately, under pressure, we are all more likely to have our stressors come out. When the stakes are high, my bad behaviors get worse. I fail to listen well because my patience is diminished. I have caught myself thinking, "If I let this person finish speaking, our company may go under tomorrow." I'm shocked at how difficult it can be to listen, especially because conceptually,

I know how to be a good listener—a great one, even. As an HR executive, most of my career has depended upon me being an adept listener.

But knowing isn't enough. We need the presence of mind to recognize when we aren't listening and then remind ourselves, "I'm not showing up at my best, and I could be damaging my relationships." When I realized my listening was declining more frequently, I made the commitment to pay attention to the circumstances leading to my diminished listening skills. If I could recognize the triggers, I could try to do better in those moments. I knew my lack of time wasn't an excuse, because when we start believing we don't have time to listen, we miss things. And what is said may very well be the thing that saves the company, or the thing that we need to hear as a manager.

Good listening is not easy or natural, especially under the stress and pressure to deliver that managers face every day. For decades, I've studied listening and the skills—focus and mindfulness—that give rise to good listening. However, even though I understand what it takes to be a good listener—from the way our hearing and our brains work to my own unconscious biases—it still requires moment-to-moment practice and intention.

Your ability to listen as a manager is directly linked to your team's performance; specifically, their engagement (or lack thereof) and their overall productivity and quality of work. It's dangerous to do too much tuning out; it will jeopardize your relationships and ultimately undermine your abilities as a leader. The skills that make a good listener are the same ones that make leaders influential and inspire the team to go above and beyond consistently in their work.

Coming to Our Senses

The good news is that among the output of the five senses (sight, hearing, touch, taste, and smell), listening is one of the few that can be improved. We generally don't think of our senses or their outputs as skills to be developed. We tend to think of them as givens, which can only be enhanced through medical interventions such as corrective lenses or hearing aids. Luckily, listening can be developed. The goal for this chapter is to provide you, the manager, with the insight, tools, and practices to improve your listening and assessing skills.

Assessing is the term I use to make sense of, or process, the input of each of the five senses. Because our senses usually just do their jobs, we don't stop to consider the role of the brain and the body in translating and organizing the data we are constantly taking in. When we assess the information coming in from our senses—the input from our ears, in this case—our brains optimize it so that we can immediately put it to use. But because we are relatively uninformed about how our own bodies and brains work, we don't realize how much of this perception is informed by our existing motivations, expectations, and beliefs. Believe it or not, our brains do the heavy lifting when it comes to translating what our senses perceive.

In December 2017, I visited the American Museum of Natural History in New York City with my son and had the opportunity to see the exhibit *Our Senses: An Immersive Experience.* I was fascinated to learn that at any given moment our brains are taking in a staggering amount of information from our senses. However, we are able to consciously process only a small fraction of that. So, while we can hear many sounds at once, we can tune in to only one sound at a time. According to this exhibit, the decision of which sound we tune in to has several factors. Conscious choice is just one. Sudden, loud sounds seize your attention because they could indicate danger. And sometimes, you notice only what you expect to hear or see.

According to ABC Science (2012), "Our ears only play part of the role in hearing; most of the really complex work is actually done by the brain." Our brains are constantly influenced by our thoughts and experiences. This is good news, because it means we can take greater responsibility for how we shape our own brains. In other words, we can become better listeners.

The fact that we hear only what we expect to hear is more complicated. Part of the reason this is so has to do with how much information the brain processes, as I mentioned. Another reason is due to unconscious bias, which we'll discuss in the "Team Dynamics of Listening" section. But a third reason concerns how well we can be present in a conversation and focus on what the speaker is trying to tell us.

The overall effectiveness of a manager's listening skills requires them to pay attention, which means they need to be able to direct and redirect their attention when their mind wanders. Given the frequency with which the average person becomes distracted, we need to constantly remind ourselves what is important to focus on. Focus and mindfulness are foundational skills, integrally linked to the emotional intelligence competencies of self-awareness and self-management. Interestingly, what we expect to hear influences what we focus on and what we actually hear.

Listening goes well beyond the mechanics of hearing itself (that is, how we physiologically process sound) and begins well before the exchange of a single word. Unfortunately, this leaves a lot of room for error, and we often get it wrong.

Listener Shortcomings and Pitfalls

Buddhist literature often references the "three defects of a vessel" when describing the incorrect ways of listening to a teaching. Not listening is to be like a vessel turned upside down. Not retaining what you hear is to be like a pot with a hole in it. And mixing negative emotions with what you hear is to be like a pot with poison in it.

As listeners, we fall short more frequently than we'd care to admit. There are numerous underlying causes for why we fail to be good listeners (and communicators for that matter). If you find yourself frequently falling prey to these listening shortcomings, it may be wise to get to the bottom of why you engage in these behaviors, along with the impact of doing so.

Here are some common listening pitfalls that managers need to be aware of. They often occur in clusters that operate at the same time within us and, in turn, compete for center stage:

1. Listening for What You Expect to Be True or Already Believe to Be True

> **Confirmation bias.** *We listen for the evidence and facts to support our existing beliefs about an event, a person, or a thing. We unconsciously listen for what we expect or want to hear.*

Impact: We aren't open to hearing, processing, or acting upon information that is different from our own perspective or that contradicts what we already believe, even if the data we receive are equally, if not more, accurate than our own.

2. Listening to Be Right or to Demonstrate Your Own Expertise

The smartest person in the room. *Some people place a high value on being right and act as if they have a monopoly on the truth. Their sole mission in life is to ensure everyone around them knows it.*

The know-it-all. *It could be because you are insecure about what you actually know and therefore are obsessed with convincing others you are right and they are wrong. Or it could be that it simply feels safer or more reassuring to know something about every possible topic that could come up, so as never to be caught flat-footed or without a point of view.*

The walking encyclopedia. *In some cases, people really are a walking reference book of random facts and know a lot about a lot of things—the more disparate and obscure, the better.*

Impact: If a person is convinced their opinion is the right or best answer, then they are less likely to listen—unless it is only to confirm that the other party agrees with them. They are likely to assert their views, argue for their opinions, and demonstrate a lack of interest in what others are saying.

3. Listening to Process or Talk

The prodigious talker. *This person fills empty spaces and does not give airtime to the other person. But while some people's predominant listening deficit is to make sure that no one else can get a word in edgewise, some are nervous talkers, and still others genuinely benefit from processing out loud or like to problem solve with varying degrees of input from others.*

Impact: Regardless of your motivation, others may eventually tune you out altogether or think you are rude for your prolonged monologue.

4. Listening Impatiently

> **The impatient listener.** *This person often interrupts and finishes other people's thoughts or sentences. This can occur when our brains are speeding ahead of what the other person is saying. Remember, our brains often are processing much more quickly than what others are saying. This can also occur if we believe we already know what the other person is trying to convey. Moreover, if we find the other person's pacing annoyingly slow or we are pressed for time, it could exacerbate this tendency.*

Impact: It causes others to feel not heard or respected and can damage your relationship with them. Additionally, because you're not really listening you may miss hearing a critical opinion or idea—one that you could benefit from hearing.

5. Listening Apathetically

> **The indifferent listener.** *This person doesn't appropriately respond; they lack curiosity or engagement with what the other person is saying. This can happen because a person is genuinely not interested in the topic, but it also occurs when they've already made a judgment about the person speaking or the topic. Consequently, they tune out what's being said because they don't think anything new or valuable will be conveyed.*

Impact: Generally speaking, you can spot an apathetic listener. It's as if the listener is looking right through you; they are not fully engaged, and it seems as if they are somewhere else. It can be pretty demoralizing, leaving the speaker feeling unappreciated, disrespected, or unheard.

6. Listening While Your Mind Wanders

> **The distracted listener.** *This person is not able to focus on what the speaker is saying. It's an acute problem today because we have so many distractions: phones, computers, social media, and the sheer volume of work we are expected to do. The stress of keeping up with so much causes us to lose focus when someone is speaking to us.*

The space cadet. *Sometimes our minds just wander. Our minds are naturally busy, thinking and feeling all kinds of things all the time.*

Impact: The person knows you're not listening because you miss what they are trying to tell you. You might ask a question they've already answered, and then suddenly they are on to you. This type of listening negatively affects the relationship.

7. Listening to Object or Take a Differing Opinion

The devil's advocate—or what I prefer to call it, the devil's applicant. *Sometimes a listener will argue because they enjoy sparring and defending their own or a differing point of view. Problems with this approach arise when objecting becomes habitual.*

The contrarian. *It doesn't matter what the speaker says; the contrarian will take an opposing point of view or a controversial stance, often correcting or pointing out the flaws of the other person's argument.*

Impact: It leaves the other person feeling unheard, disrespected, and unable to fully present an idea before having it shot down, corrected, or debated.

8. Listening to Poke Holes or Look for Inconsistencies

The fault finder. *Often this can be the downfall of someone who is facts or data driven, or someone who is pressed for time. If someone is presenting an idea, instead of getting curious and asking questions, their first reaction is to find fault or to point out what's wrong with the idea. Generally, they don't realize they're doing this, and their intentions aren't always bad—in fact, often they're good. Usually, it's because they want something to succeed and have a genuine concern for the approach being taken.*

Impact: This behavior can be demoralizing and demotivating, and it can cause others around you to disengage. The rougher the delivery, the more this is true. People will find ways to work around you and get things done without your input. They might look you in the eye and tell you exactly what you want to hear, and then go do exactly what they want to do.

✳ ✳ ✳

We all engage in these poor listening habits to varying degrees. A first good step to remedying your poor listening habits is setting your intention for the relationship with the person you're listening to. In fact, you could argue that listening and assessing require our ability to pay attention vis à vis our other senses. If someone isn't speaking but their body language and gestures are telling a story, then our ability to notice these interpersonal nuances becomes important. Facial expressions, tone of voice, and speaking volume also give us direct clues about how the other person is feeling.

Our capacity as managers to be good listeners depends on our ability to consistently engage in both intrapersonal and interpersonal skills.

Intrapersonal Listening Skills

Becoming a good listener begins with understanding your strengths and weaknesses in the following emotional intelligence competencies: self-awareness, focus, mindfulness, and self-management. These skills are foundational to how we interact with others—our interpersonal aptitude—which we will discuss in the next section.

Intrapersonal skills are important because they exist as capabilities within each of us; these are skills we can draw from to be more effective in our lives and in our relationships. Intrapersonal skills are what we have the ability to influence at the most basic level within ourselves. In any given conversation, we can strive to focus on the other person and be mindful of our verbal and nonverbal communication, but we can't control these elements in the other person. We can't regulate what they say, what they think, what they do, or how they react emotionally.

The following are tools, including questions you can ask yourself, to evaluate whether you are tapping into the intrapersonal skills needed to be a competent and adept listener.

Self-Awareness

Effective relationships and communication depend on our self-awareness. How can we control our impulses and emotional reactions if we are not aware of them? While there are many layers of meaning around self-awareness, it is simply the capacity that we all have to be attentive and notice not only what's going on around us, but what's happening and unfolding within our own experience. Self-awareness means that we are cognizant of our perceptions, emotions, and almost-instantaneous interpretation of our experience in the moment.

For example, my friend Lauren is a sales manager in a large organization. She happens to be very self-aware. She can generally recognize and understand her own emotions and resets quickly when presented with a challenge or obstacle. When we met for dinner one evening, she told me about her day, which had been a particularly rough one. She'd been double booked for her first morning meeting and was running to catch up the rest of the day. By midmorning, someone on her team quit unexpectedly because of a conflict with another team member and wanted to speak to Lauren immediately. Lauren was already feeling rushed and anxious, but she cleared her schedule to meet with the woman on her team. Before she did, however, Lauren took a few seconds to sit quietly and take three intentional and full breaths.

"I had to make sure I reset before I met with her," Lauren told me later, "or else I probably would have still been frazzled by being overbooked and I wouldn't have been attentive to her needs in the moment. She was already so upset she wanted to quit. I knew I had to be calm and present with her. As a leader, all eyes are on me. I can't afford to be off-center."

Lauren had enough self-awareness to recognize her state of mind and knew that to be her best, she needed a moment to reset. At dinner, after telling me the story, Lauren was able to shrug off the challenges of the day.

"Everyone has a bad day every now and again," she said. Her awareness that her emotions are normal and common is also a component of healthy self-awareness. She was able to recognize that events and other people's emotions are out of our immediate control. In fact, we can't be sure who else on our team might be having a rough day. Starting every meeting with a 60-second sit or by taking three deep breaths, similar to how Lauren reset before her meeting, allows people a moment to reset and focus upon the task at hand.

Here are some questions to ask yourself about your self-awareness:

- Am I cognizant of my thoughts, emotions, perceptions, and judgments? Are my emotions getting the best of me?
- Is my judgment of the other person or what they're saying getting in the way?
- Are my biases, whether consciously or unconsciously derived, acting as a barrier or filter, preventing me from hearing, processing, or understanding what the other person is saying?

Focus

Everyone understands what it means to focus, but unfortunately today we all experience a lack of focus. We are incredibly distracted by our external environment, not to mention the fact that our minds wander when we are unable to keep our attention on the desired target. Mind wandering can also take the form of "inner chatter," or a steady flow of thoughts, feelings, and mental impressions that unfolds in the backdrop of our awareness.

It turns out we have circuitry in the brain that allows us to selectively focus our attention. We can bring our attention to a single point, like on our breath. Or we can do the opposite: We can have a broad, open awareness. We can even have an awareness of awareness itself—referred to as meta-cognition. What we pay attention to becomes our immediate reality, for better or for worse. For example, imagine you're listening to a presentation and you're asked to count the number of times the speaker says "um." You might strike the correct number of tally marks, but you're probably not going to hear what else was said. Where we focus—consciously or unconsciously—colors everything else: our perceptions, our assessments, even what we hear. While focus is not an emotional intelligence competency, it is a fundamental skill, an aspect of self-awareness. When having a conversation, it's important to ask yourself, "Am I distracted in this moment?"

But there's another aspect to focus. We can be focused, but on the wrong thing. I used to work with a manager of business development, whose job was to bring in new business for the company. But, years earlier, he had been a design student and worked for several years in advertising as a graphic designer. So, while he should have spent his day on the phone and in meetings with prospective clients, he'd spend hours at his desk creating PowerPoint presentations. The idea was that these were for the client meetings, but his focus was clearly on the design, rather than getting in front of as many clients as possible. We often focus on what we're most interested in doing or what we already have proficiency in, and we tend to avoid aspects of our work in which we have little to no interest or areas in which we don't have experience. A good manager will ask not only, "Am I focused?" but "Am I focused on the right things?"

While managers don't have direct control over what their team members focus upon, they should do what they can to check in and ensure they are on track directionally. On a practical level, they can increase their team's focus by modeling good listening and attention practices—putting away cell phones and laptops, for example—and asking others to do the same. Minimizing distractions is an easy step toward creating the conditions for focus. Email can also be a distraction throughout our workday. A lot of people, myself included, go right to email as opposed to setting it aside and getting other important work done.

Here are some questions to ask yourself about your focus:

- Am I focused on what the person is saying? Or am I thinking about what I am going to say next, or something else entirely?
- Is my mind wandering?

Mindfulness

Being mindful keeps us on track. It's that aspect of our mind that can remind us not to react to our triggers. For example, when someone cuts us off in traffic, mindfulness is like an emissary of self-awareness encouraging us to stay calm and not fly off the handle.

Mindfulness, in this context, is not the mindfulness that we hear of in the mainstream mindfulness movement. Here we're tapping into the origins of the word *mindfulness*: *sati* in Pali, which translates to "memory," and *smrti* in Sanskrit, which means "to remember, to recollect, or to bear in mind." It's the aspect of our mind that can maintain a line of sight toward what's most important in any given moment.

Being mindful is invaluable when listening. Maybe you need to remind yourself that you're not going to interrupt a direct report while they're talking, for example. When you realize you're distracted, you recall the need to stay focused on what another person is saying.

For example, Ben is a task-oriented manager, who prioritizes milestones and goal achievement over spending time to connect with his team. He starts all his meetings by going straight to the numbers, ignoring personal chatter. By employing mindfulness, Ben can remind himself of the value of allowing team members to connect with one another. Even though his natural inclination is to get straight to the point, the people around him have different needs. Effective managers acknowledge these differences.

So, perhaps in the next meeting, instead of immediately jumping into the business at hand, he could suggest that his team go around the table and share, "What's on top?" He can lead with questions that allow team members to connect with themselves and one another, such as "What's inspiring you today?" "What makes you hopeful about today?" "What got you up this morning?" It could be even just be, "Share one or two words about how you're feeling." The point is to demonstrate genuine care and appreciation for the team.

Here are some questions to ask yourself about your mindfulness:
- Am I able to keep a line of sight toward those actions and behaviors that allow me to show up at my best?
- Am I able to practice tactics of being a good listener?

Self-Management

Self-management is interchangeable with emotional balance. It speaks to our ability to navigate our impulses and emotional reactions and course-correct when we go off track. Our brains are constantly shaped by our experiences and our thoughts. When we engage in contemplative practices that strengthen our self-awareness, focus, and emotional balance, we're essentially training our brains. We are much better poised to manage our reactions and our impulses if we are operating from a strong foundation of self-awareness.

For managers, this might take the form of maintaining your cool under pressure. For example, one day I had three people come to me within five minutes of one another, each with an emergency requiring my immediate attention. I began to feel stressed, but instead of letting irritation creep in and affect my behavior, I managed my emotional response. I recognized that I was feeling upset, so rather than snapping at the third person to knock on my door, I took a breath and remembered to stay calm. These crises weren't created by my team members, and it wasn't their fault that they happened all at once. Although it was a long day, I was able to manage my reactions, and even at home, I remembered not to snap at my family just because I'd had a rough day. Another common reaction to stress is to shut down. With self-management, we can persevere even in trying moments.

Self-management involves pushing past the knee-jerk need to react and instead to make sure that every interaction you have leaves the other person feeling respected and heard.

Here are some questions to ask yourself about your self-management:
- Am I managing and regulating my impulses and emotions?
- By regulating my emotions, am I better able to manage my responses in a skillful and context-appropriate manner?

✳ ✳ ✳

Self-awareness, focus, mindfulness, and self-management are connected, as illustrated in Figure 5-1. Focus can lead to mindfulness, which can lead to self-management, in that moment. By remembering to pay attention—and listen—you can manage your reactions to situations.

Figure 5-1. Intrapersonal Gears

If we can be mindful and something catches us off guard, the likelihood of us returning to center more quickly is much greater. Looking at it from another angle, I would argue that it's not possible to manage your impulses and reactions if you're not self-aware.

Interpersonal Listening Skills

In contrast with intrapersonal listening, *interpersonal listening* refers to listening skills we employ to genuinely connect with and tune into others. For example, the ability to read body language and facial expressions accurately or pay attention to cues as a means of tuning in to the other person's state of mind.

But before we address the various interpersonal skills involved with listening, let's do a quick review of the types of listening that leadership and therapeutic communities have taught for years. *Reflective listening* is a communication strategy involving two key steps: seeking to understand a speaker's idea, then offering the idea back to the speaker to confirm you understand it correctly. For example, "What I hear you saying is that the data are unclear, and you need additional resources to finish the report. Is that correct?" *Active listening* requires that the listener pays full attention and demonstrates understanding of what the speaker has said.

To both of these listening strategies, we can add asking thoughtful questions, demonstrating curiosity about what the speaker is saying. So much of what makes a person feel heard and understood is knowing the other person is interested in what they are talking about—engaged and asking well-placed questions. Here are some additional skills necessary for successful interpersonal listening.

Empathic Attunement

Empathic attunement takes listening skills to a whole new level of sophistication. It's a term that has its roots in psychoanalysis; nonetheless, it fits beautifully within the context of being a skillful listener. "In empathic attunement, one tries to respond to the [speaker's] perception of reality at that moment, as opposed to one's own or some 'objective' or external view of what is real," wrote psychotherapists Leslie S. Greenberg, Laura N. Rice, and Robert Elliott (1993) in *Facilitating Emotional Change* (quoted in Finlay 2015). Empathic attunement combines reflective and active components of listening and adds empathy, allowing the speaker to feel heard, understood, and genuinely connected to the listener. By employing empathic attunement, we can circumvent any mechanical tendencies we might have when demonstrating our understanding of what the other person has said and instead fully tune into what they have said. According to integrative psychotherapist and academic consultant Linda Finlay (2015), "When we empathically attune to another we gently tune into, sense, and resonate with their experience."

For example, let's say that Robert goes to meet with his manager, Sandra, and she can tell that something's wrong. So, she asks, "What's going on?" Robert tells her, "My cat is ill."

Sandra might respond in a manner that acknowledges what he has told her. She may even conceptually feel badly for Robert, remembering when her dog Mr. Tootles fell ill. But unless she shows genuine care for Robert in that moment, her response may feel perfunctory or even disingenuous.

By contrast, when we empathically connect with the other person, it comes through as a heartfelt moment. As a manager, it's important to connect with your team members on a genuine foundation of care, beyond just their performance in the office. Empathic attunement is tapping into the feelings of another person and allowing them to sense that you care. That care might take the form of allowing them to step back from an immediate deliverable or giving the person enough space to work through their emotions while you provide the ground cover and space for them to recover emotionally.

According to Daniel Goleman's work, there are three different kinds of empathy. At the cognitive level, we can recognize when a person is in a favorable or an unfavorable position; we may even feel bad for them, but we're not emotionally connecting with their situation. It's mostly an intellectual exercise, where you can observe somebody else's situation and say, "Oh, that's not good for that person." For example, if Lisa got a negative performance review or her sales numbers were low, you might think, "That stinks for Lisa." That's a conceptual kind of empathy that may not be particularly heartfelt.

When we practice emotional empathy, we put ourselves in the other person's shoes and can understand what they are going through, based on how we imagine it might feel to be in their position.

Finally, there is a third layer of empathy called empathic concern. This is when we demonstrate genuine care and concern for another person, which can often be missing from a manager's concerted efforts to cultivate empathy. And yet it is precisely this kind of care that causes people to invest in the relationship and the work you do together. You can't fake this level of care.

In terms of interpersonal listening skills, empathy allows you to connect with the other person in a way that builds the relationship. For example, if you don't see the other person as worthy of being heard, or if you don't consider their ideas valuable enough to listen to, chances are you're not going to be a very good listener. Conversely, when you do value what someone has to say and their point of view, they are going to feel that from you. And as a good friend of mine always says, none of us is as good actor as we think we are. If you're speaking with somebody you don't like, even if you put on the pretense you think you should, they can still detect your true feelings because emotions are contagious—for better or worse. Faking empathy doesn't work; in fact, it will eventually backfire. It's important to develop genuine empathy and go beyond cognitive empathy to really connect with the other person. Somebody who is not empathetic will struggle with the interpersonal side of listening.

Social Awareness

Social awareness is the ability to tune into how the other person is feeling and adjust your own perspective accordingly. Listening isn't done exclusively through the faculty of hearing; you read nonverbal cues and facial expressions using different areas in the brain. For some people these skills come naturally; for others, not so much. Either way, we can work to develop these skills. Social awareness also depends on having self-awareness; we have to recognize our emotions and their impact on us as well as those with whom we're interacting.

While we can try our best to read these cues, we don't always get it right. Sometimes we need to double-check our impressions and assumptions. As a manager, if you're not sure how someone is feeling, you should ask: "I'm sensing that you're a little down. Am I off base? Feel free to correct me if I'm wrong." Check in with the person when you sense something is off, even if they haven't necessarily said it. Or let's say you're on the phone with a direct report and discussing a project, but you sense that they're not into it. Somebody who's not socially aware would just keep going, whereas somebody who is would say, "I want to take a step back. I realize I'm doing most of the talking. Do you have any questions or anything you'd like to say?" Pause to check in with others, especially in the absence of clear data about how they're doing.

Alignment of Purpose

Listening helps us get to the heart of why we are talking with another person. But often—in fact, most of the time—when we enter into a conversation, we don't stop to consider our objectives for that conversation, let alone the other person's expectations for the dialogue. This can lead to problems. For example, you may believe the direct report you're speaking with wants a solution to the dilemma they're describing. But really, all they want is to be heard and possibly encouraged. The conversation will likely feel frustrating to you both if you don't clarify expectations.

When possible, identify the purpose of the conversation and align your outcomes: "Why are we having this dialogue? What are your expectations? What are mine?" Then, work together toward the outcomes you have in common. Establishing these parameters up front can help bypass a lot of the pitfalls that happen in communication. It can help to avoid misunderstandings; when conflict does arise, returning to these three questions can help reopen the dialogue.

For example, imagine you forgot to establish the goals of the conversation up front and it gets off to a rocky start. You start to sense the other person is uncomfortable, and you're feeling uncomfortable, too. Stop and request permission to take a step back: "I'm sorry. I realize I failed to ask some really important questions." Ask the questions, listen to the answers, and try to agree on your intentions. Then, continue with the dialogue. Aligning the conversation outcomes is a problem even in close relationships. We think that because we know the other person, we don't have to go through these steps. But, perhaps especially with people we know well, these questions would save us a lot of heartburn.

Good interpersonal listening involves consciously identifying what you believe the conversation is about and your role relative to that purpose. The beliefs we hold about the purpose of any given dialogue determine how we listen as managers. They also determine how we engage our direct reports and colleagues as we listen to them. If we head into conversations before considering these factors, we will be blind to the underlying mechanisms at play and might fall back on whatever tendencies we already have.

In short, the quality and nature of our listening is inextricably linked to why we believe we are having the conversation to begin with. While this is not an exhaustive list, we often engage in dialogue to achieve one or more of the following objectives:

- Impart your point of view.
- Influence an outcome.
- Assert authority or control.
- Demonstrate a level of understanding or expertise.
- Hear yourself talk, either to make sense of what you think out loud, or with no other purpose beyond that.
- Win approval.
- Transmit knowledge.
- Gain agreement or consensus.
- Find common ground or a mutual purpose.
- Inspire others.
- Understand the other person's point of view.
- Gain greater knowledge about a topic.
- Try out an idea.
- Problem solve.
- Pass the time.
- Ask for support, help, or advice.

The more skillful you are, the more likely you will achieve your aims and:

- Effectively listen to others.
- Respond in a context-appropriate manner.
- Ask relevant follow-up questions.
- Express your point of view only after you have fully heard and understood the other person's point of view.

However, if you lack skill as a listener or communicator, there is a good chance you probably aren't listening well or only long enough to assert your point of view, or you are preoccupied with what your response will be.

Team Dynamics of Listening

Listening is only one part of team dynamics, albeit an important one. It sits within a bigger backdrop of establishing team norms—what Vanessa Druskat defines as "the habits, expectations, and behaviors of a team." A good manager will look at team norms honestly and critically and then discuss them with the group, including how well they listen to one another.

Use the assessment in the appendix to understand individual listening habits, and then to help establish positive group-listening norms. It is well worth a manager's time to assess individual norms, including their own, as well as team norms. The manager, first and foremost, has to go through the steps of becoming self-aware. We've all been in meetings where no one seems to be listening to one another: One person may never stop talking, another talks only to beat a dead horse, another seems too shy to contribute, and another is clearly engaged in a separate activity. This group could benefit from a manager who is tuned in to these dynamics and actively engages the team to reflect on their own habits and whether they are serving them well. A manager who is self-aware will evaluate their own listening and communication style and adjust to fit the needs and norms of the team. It's important to have the entire team reflect upon the kinds of listening habits they are contributing to the group dynamic.

Unconscious Bias

Everyone has unconscious bias. Even if we consciously think, "I'm going to try to be as objective as possible," the way our senses process incoming data inevitability creates bias; it's part of how our brains process and organize input. We can't process all incoming data, so there are gaps and imperfections to what we take in; our brains then fill in what our senses miss. In other words, our expectations of how a conversation will go and our pre-existing concepts influence what we focus on, what we see and hear, and how we process those data points. To develop positive team norms, your group needs to be aware of the role unconscious bias plays in how we make sense of what we perceive.

Unconscious bias takes many forms, including confirmation bias. In confirmation bias, we listen for evidence that supports what we already believe. We inadvertently focus on the information that supports our point of view, diminishing or tuning out certain facts that don't validate our point of view. It turns out that our existing beliefs and expectations actually shape what we think and, in turn, the meaning we make of what we perceive—in this case, what we hear.

Leonard Mlodinow (2012), an American theoretical physicist who has written about the role of the unconscious mind and subliminal processes, offers a metaphor to describe two common lenses people use in their interpersonal interactions: that of an attorney's or a scientist's. An attorney starts with the end goal in mind and works backward, drawing upon those elements that help build and bolster the argument or case. The scientist is looking for truth, and uses facts to formulate theories and draw conclusions. Each is unconsciously molding the information to best fit their respective paradigm.

Within team dynamics, this gets more complicated, with each individual listening with their own filters and lenses in place. Awareness is key: If a person goes into conversations knowing about unconscious bias, they can try to mitigate its effect on their listening skills and interpretation of what they've heard. A manager can also establish norms that take the existing team dynamics into consideration. For example, they may ask team members to take a position they normally wouldn't support. If a team member is a facts-driven person who has a habit of poking holes in other people's ideas, particularly if they're missing some of their facts, the manager might say to them privately, "I know this is your go-to, and we love that you are always looking for ways to ensure our success, but today I want you to ask questions in such a way that allows others to see any gaps that could get in the way of desired results" or "Today, we're going to focus on unrestrained creativity, and we'll double back and discuss feasibility at a later date." This will hopefully allow this individual to see things from a new perspective.

Influence

Influence within the group is another consideration. Senior leaders usually wield influence, but so can anyone in the group who has power, either formally (through titles) or informally (by their ability to influence decisions). Sometimes the person with the most influence is just the loudest voice. Often, the norms of a team coincide with the preferences and habits of formal and informal leaders, which is not necessarily the path that will lead to the team's overall success. A skilled manager will discern where there is a bias toward certain types of voices or ways of communicating.

Let's say the head of legal is often invited to be part of important team discussions, yet no matter what gets discussed, even strategy and innovation, the filter is one of risk aversion. Depending on that individual's level of influence and control, this filter could drown out other valuable points of view. It can be demotivating for team members to have to defer to one or two lenses (usually the leaders') most of the time. The group is then expected to "paint inside the lines" and adhere to whatever the preferred perspectives might be—often to the detriment of hearing all the voices around the table and seeing the bigger picture along with what is needed to achieve the desired results.

By recognizing individual listening norms and, as a team, crafting group-listening norms, the team can begin to bring self-awareness to its discussions. To that end, teams can ask the following questions:

- Do we have listening norms?
- Do the individual norms of informal or formal leaders tend to overshadow or dictate the team norms?
- Do we have a listening culture that closes out valuable voices that represent our diversity as a team?

What Good Listening Looks Like on a Team

First of all, if you and your team are talking about group norms and biases—or even about being better listeners—that's a great start. Teams who actively welcome different, even conflicting, perspectives tend to see conflict as an opportunity to learn about someone else's point of view, ask better questions, and truly embrace and incorporate others' ideas.

Engage in these types of experiments as a team and be transparent about it. Tell your people, "Teams are complex, and we are no exception. We're going to establish some norms around tolerance of conflict, the ability to talk about what's working and what isn't, and how to take a different yet respectful stance." People need permission to do that without fear of negative consequences.

Leaders who are either closed off to other points of view or conflict averse will often not see the value of eliciting conflicting viewpoints. Moreover, leaders who employ a command and control style of leadership often aren't able to receive the candid feedback that would let them know how others feel about them. Their direct reports not only will hesitate to provide vital input in this regard, but also won't volunteer their ideas due to their lack of trust in how that information will be handled or for fear of being reprimanded or losing their job.

To ensure a greater balance of listening, managers can change the meeting structure. Instead of having an open exchange of dialogue in which the same people are weighing in, they can suggest a round-robin approach, where the team goes around the table and listens to each person's input. Or, managers can take a facilitator's role in the meeting, meaning they ensure everyone has an opportunity to weigh in and the group follows agreed-upon norms. They focus on bringing the group to a consensus, rather than doing most of the speaking. In other words, managers should be quiet to ensure other people's voices are heard.

Strategies to Improve Listening

While some people are naturally good listeners, others are not. Poor listening skills affect your efficacy as a manager and are worth improving. Luckily, there are a number of ways to do that.

Improving Intrapersonal Listening Skills

There are certain practices that allow us to strengthen the neural connections in our brains that are responsible for self-awareness and focus (or attention).

Training for the Brain

One of the best strategies to increase your self-awareness, focus, and mindfulness is to engage in attention-training practices such as The Body Scan and Awareness of Breath. It's like how you might go to the gym if you want to increase your core strength.

According to Richard Davidson, professor of psychology and psychiatry at the University of Wisconsin–Madison, resilience is the rapidity with which we can recover from a setback. We all have different set-points that determine how readily we are triggered and how long it takes us to recover when we encounter an obstacle, whether it be an actual or a perceived threat. There is a neural highway running between the prefrontal cortex (PFC), which regulates complex cognitive, emotional, and behavioral functions (higher-level thinking), and the amygdala, which is responsible, in part, for our fight or flight mechanism (more primitive thinking). When we are hijacked by emotional events or social threats—say, a disruptive outburst from a direct report or the perception we are being treated unfairly—if we have a stronger connection between the PFC and amygdala, we can bounce back more quickly. The PFC down regulates the amygdala more quickly, allowing us to regain composure, calm down, and manage our reactions more adeptly.

Certain contemplative practices have demonstrated the ability to strengthen this neural connection between the PFC and the amygdala. In a 2008 study, Davidson and his team took a group of people who weren't meditators and asked them to do a daily, 30-minute meditation based on compassion. After two weeks, they showed physical changes in their brain structures compared with the fMRI images taken before the study began. Their behavior changed as well. Each participant was given a sum of money and the choice to keep it or spend it on another person, in a practice called The Redistribution Game. When given an opportunity to demonstrate compassion, they did (Lutz et al. 2008).

We don't have to be part of a research study to strengthen our own connections; however, it does take consistent practice. Here is an abbreviated version of compassion practice, the full version of which can be found on the Center for Healthy Minds website (2016):

> *Call to mind someone you are close to who may be going through a life struggle or some kind of crisis at the moment or someone who you simply care about a great deal. Visualize this person clearly in your mind's eye, and then offer them the following:*

- *May you be free of suffering and the causes of suffering.*
- *May you have happiness and the causes of happiness.*

Now, call to mind someone you feel neutral about, could be a neighbor or a co-worker you don't know quite as well, and offer them the same:

- *May you be free of suffering and the causes of suffering.*
- *May you have happiness and the causes of happiness.*

Now, call to mind someone you actively struggle with, visualizing someone specific with whom you have experienced some conflict, and wish them the same:

- *May you be free of suffering and the causes of suffering.*
- *May you have happiness and the causes of happiness.*

Now call to mind yourself and say:

- *May I be free of suffering and the causes of suffering.*
- *May I have happiness and the causes of happiness.*

Finally, call to mind all beings, and offer the following:

- *May all beings be free of suffering and the causes of suffering.*
- *May all beings have happiness and the causes of happiness.*

Set Intentions

A second strategy for improving intrapersonal listening skills is to set intentions or listening objectives. You can start by completing the assessment in the appendix and identifying some of your listening pitfalls—interrupting others, for example. Then, form a strong, positively framed intention around what it is you'd rather do and why: "When I interrupt my colleagues, it causes them to feel that I don't respect them and it's demotivating." When you understand the impact of how you behave, you can begin to see the consequences of how you're showing up.

Part of what really matters when forming intentions is not to gloss over the impact of poor listening, but to internalize the significance of continuing down that path. The thought process is important here: "If I keep interrupting, letting my mind wander, or closing myself off to any input, here are the likely outcomes." I have found that people who can spot the causal relationship between their behaviors, actions, and results are able to form a resolve that is more likely to stick. And that resolve, in turn, directly links to our ability to stay mindful and on track. The more we care about something—the more interested we are in doing it—the more likely we will remember to do it in the heat of the moment.

Practice Self-Awareness

Finally, building self-awareness improves our intrapersonal listening skills. Give yourself a visual reminder; write yourself a note that you can see first thing in the morning that says, "Today, I'm going to focus on listening instead of talking. I'll ask questions instead of telling. I'm going to try coming off of autopilot and pay attention with a certain quality of mindfulness and awareness that allows me to operate at my best." I've also coached people who have come up with some visual reminder to stay mindful, such as wearing a rubber band around their wrist.

Throughout the day, ask yourself how you're doing. How did you show up today? How did you do relative to how you'd like to behave? In other words, did you conduct yourself in a way that represented how you want to be and that represents you at your best? Going through an intentional inventory of how things went throughout the day and journaling about it, or even just thinking about it, builds the habit of cognitive self-awareness.

✳ ✳ ✳

Applying these practices—setting intentions and applying micro-techniques that strengthen our self-awareness—in our day-to-day lives as often as we can will move the needle for us. If it remains an idea on a page, it won't change anything.

Improving Interpersonal Listening Skills

Strengthening our own self-awareness is foundational to how we listen to others. If we lack self-awareness, then we may not know how we are being experienced and perceived by those we interact with. This could impede our relationships, not to mention our outcomes.

Get 360 Feedback

Start with a good understanding of how others perceive you. As a manager, it's important to get a clear understanding of how effective you are at listening and reading people. Ideally, it would be a measure of your emotional intelligence, obtaining direct input from others who are close to you, not only people you work with but friends and family members, too. Getting that 360 perspective is an essential starting place. It lets you know how good your interpersonal skills are and where you need to focus your efforts to improve. Make sure, however, you choose a 360 instrument that is validated.

Work With a Coach

We don't know what we don't know about ourselves. Often we need somebody who has our best interests at heart and can help us see ourselves more clearly. A coach can work with you one-on-one to help you see what's holding you back. They might come to a meeting to observe your interactions with others and give you real-time feedback. While you're experimenting with new behaviors and practices to be a better listener, you might want somebody to observe and ask, "How do you think that went? What would you do differently next time?"

Finding Your Motivation

Developing interpersonal listening skills depends on how motivated we are to change, and how much we care. Often, how much we care is directly related to our perception of impact. If I perceive that the stakes are low, and I'm not particularly interested in self-improvement for self-improvement purposes alone, then my interest level is likely to be quite low. Yet because changing habits is neither quick nor easy, intrinsic motivation is key for following through.

It's often the case that the people who need to improve the most also need help finding a reason to shift their habits. Sometimes it takes a leader almost derailing before they realize the gravity of the situation and think, "I need to wake up and pay attention." Unfortunately, by the time a leader gets one of those wake-up calls—and it's not the kind of call anybody likes to get—their job could be in jeopardy. I've seen it come in the form of a manager being told, "Shape up or ship out. You've got 30 days to improve." Until someone helps connect the dots between poor listening skills and the effects on their relationships and results, they often will have a hard time getting motivated enough to make the needed changes.

Not surprisingly, this largely comes back to self-awareness and focus. You can't be a good manager if your attention is wandering, if you aren't aware, or if you are tuning in to the wrong things. Ultimately, our interpersonal skills are tied to our intrapersonal skills, the latter of which are foundational for not only being an excellent listener but also developing any leadership competencies whatsoever.

Strategies to Get Back on Track

Remember that our brains immediately set to work making sense of the information our senses are capturing, including what we hear. When we are triggered by something that another person has said, it can be our signal that we need to adjust. In practical terms, what does this look like?

We can be triggered by something a person says or does that upsets us. Triggers can be an external obstacle or, more often, an emotional hijack. But before you gravitate toward a go-to reaction, such as tuning the other person out, poking holes in their ideas, withdrawing, or lashing out, the trigger itself can serve as a reminder to pause, regain composure, and exercise restraint. That trigger is like a call to action in the moment to notice and assess your own behavior. Sometimes, it could be a reminder that causes us to pause and realize, "I'm not being a good listener right now. If I say or do this thing, it's going to damage my relationship with this person." Getting back on track in these moments requires you to develop self-awareness. It is your presence of mind in that moment that allows you to spot and deal more skillfully with your unproductive or destructive emotions. At the moment you realize you have gone off track or are about to, you can redirect yourself instead.

Pivoting allows us to recover from a setback. Pivoting is the process of noticing and working with the thing that has triggered us, and then moving toward better habits, such as employing better listening skills.

What happens in our brains when we pivot? The prefrontal cortex down regulates the amygdala, causing us to become unstuck, let go, and move on. You can strengthen the neural pathway between the PFC and amygdala by consistently practicing different types of microtechniques, such as meditation with focus. Training the brain in this way allows you to pivot more quickly when faced with adversity.

Noticing that you've been triggered is your signal to come back to your core intent; re-engage in the dialogue and listen well; notice any filters, judgment, or bias that you have in that moment; and bring an open mind to the conversation.

Good listening involves tuning in to your internal state as well as that of the other person. We generally communicate what we want the other person to know, even if we're not consciously aware of it. So, pay attention. We're always speaking to each other. However, if you are not paying attention to the other person's feelings, you may miss the story that's unfolding right before you.

Moreover, if you go into a conversation and you're off emotionally, the other person will likely "catch" your emotional state and feel what you are feeling. But if you can pause and notice your emotional state, you can take a moment to readjust your mindset so as not to influence the other person.

You can also remember to attune yourself to others' feelings in the moment and be poised to respond with a greater level of care and skill. You can better perceive their emotions and, in turn, take measures to prevent your emotional state from negatively affecting others. Attunement depends on self-awareness and social awareness. Remind yourself which listening strategy is most needed in this moment. Applying the appropriate remedy from the list of intrapersonal or interpersonal listening strategies and tuning in to the other person's internal state increases the odds of being an effective listener.

Here are some additional strategies to practice in daily conversations to improve listening skills. You can also teach these strategies to your team members to help increase their listening skills.

- Before you begin a conversation, take a few deep breaths, try to center, and focus your attention on why you're having the discussion. Set your intention to be a good listener. Tell yourself, "I need to set aside my preoccupations and distractions for this moment. I need to let go of them to be fully present with this person and truly listen."

- To avoid the pitfalls of unconscious bias, ask yourself, "What do I believe about the person or topic at hand? Am I gathering evidence to support my existing point of view?" If you have a good relationship with the other person, beware that you could be agreeing with them on that basis versus what they are saying. If you do not have a good relationship, your feelings could similarly cloud your perspective.

- When listening to someone with whom you disagree, try to find points of agreement and synergy. Open yourself to other people's ideas even when you think they might be wrong. Let others state their ideas completely, and refrain from jumping in with an immediate response or judgment. Take a step back and tell yourself there's an opportunity to learn a new perspective.

- Fight the urge to be right. Let others shine and have the floor, even if you disagree with them. In fact, especially if you disagree, ask for their opinion or advice on the topic. Shift the purpose of the conversation from being right or having a dominant point of view to asking questions to promote dialogue. Instead of making a mark on this conversation based on what you know, make a mark by ensuring the other person feels heard.

- When listening to someone who you think has a weak or unsubstantiated point of view, resist the urge to poke holes in what they are saying. Instead of approaching the conversation as a fact-finding mission, approach it as if you would like to learn something. Or, you could rephrase the way you look for additional information. Instead of saying, "That's not going to work," say, "I want to support what you're proposing, but I'm concerned about the outcome. I want to make sure we're thinking about the following things."

- If you feel you need to think out loud, explain your intent to the other person and seek their permission to use them as a human sounding board. Also, try limiting yourself to a certain amount of time to talk nonstop. Break it up into manageable, one- to three-minute sessions. You could also try recording yourself speaking, or journaling to explore your thoughts.

- If you think you know what the other person is trying to say, don't interrupt. Challenge yourself to let the other person continue speaking. You can even check to see how often you were right—you did know what they were going to say—or wrong—they said something different than what you expected.

- If the conversation involves a topic you're not interested in, first dispense with any preconceived notions, and ask questions to keep yourself engaged. Try to find some aspect of what the speaker is saying that sparks your curiosity. If it's a topic you don't know much about, don't be afraid to ask very basic questions. Often, we become bored with what somebody is saying because we don't know how to bridge our understanding. Asking good questions helps.

- If you find your attention wandering, pretend you have to explain what this person has said to somebody else, or that you have to write an article on the topic. In other words, trick your brain. Tell yourself, "If I were asked to recap what this person has said, I'd have to really understand the crux of what they're trying to tell me. I need to get super curious about this, just for the moment." And then, fully listen.

- If you can't get interested in what they're saying, remind yourself of your intentions for this relationship. Are you interested in building or maintaining the relationship with the other person? At a minimum, at least be interested in the fact that if you don't listen to them they are going to feel your apathy, which will damage the relationship.

Summary

Listening is an everyday skill managers need in their arsenal, one that is often neglected in the command and control and pace-setting leadership styles. For too long, managers have been expected to have answers. However, with the ACCEL framework built around managers who serve not as overseers but as developers of talent, managers now have permission to talk less and listen more.

I'll wrap up with a story around the phrase "empty your cup," which is attributed to a conversation between a teacher, Zen Master Ryutan, and a student, Tokusan. Tokusan, who was full of knowledge and opinions, came to Ryutan and asked about Zen. Ryutan is said to have refilled his guest's teacup but did not stop pouring when the cup was full. Tea spilled out and ran over the table. "Stop! The cup is full!" said Tokusan.

Similarly, you can use the metaphor of a cup, and this chapter, to examine the quality of your own listening:

- **Is your cup too full?** Do you lack the openness to accept any new information?
- **Is your cup upside down?** Are you closed off to what is being said, due to either a lack of focus or a lack of openness?
- **Is your cup dirty?** Are views or beliefs contaminating what's being said or your ability to understand? Do you have a bias that is preventing you from hearing what the other person has to say?
- **Is your cup cracked?** Is your inability to focus preventing your from listening or retaining information?

Appendix
Templates and Resources

The following section contains templates and resources for you to use as you implement the ACCEL model.

- FACES of Accountability
- Creating Fun Environments
- The Collaboration Operating Platform
- Your Preference for Collaboration?
- What Does Collaboration Look Like for You?
- Theory X—Theory Y
- Rate Your Proficiency With the Collaboration Competencies
- Manager Engagement Worksheet
- Listening and Assessment Styles and Habits Self-Assessment

FACES of Accountability

Managers are responsible (and accountable) for continuing to develop their staff. Use this job aid as a quarterly accountability checklist for your direct reports. Fill out the activity, outcome, and next steps for each activity related to this pillar of the ACCEL framework.

	Quarterly Activity	Outcome?	Next Steps?
F			
A			
C			
E			
S			

Creating Fun Environments

To find out if your team is fun, answer the questions below. Three or more yeses means your team is having a good time!

Is Your Team Fun?

Are your direct reports regularly smiling or laughing?

    Yes   No

Does your team or organization regularly have fun activities?

    Yes   No

Do you or your team acknowledge when something is funny?

    Yes   No

Are members of your team friends?

    Yes   No

Do your team members talk about non-work-related topics?

    Yes   No

Create a Culture of Fun

Define what is (and is not) acceptable

- Pranks, sexual humor, and any other jokes that are offensive should be avoided

Ask about their lives

- Ask about their weekend
- Ask about family (spouse, kids, etc.) and friends

Add fun to meetings

- Share fun stories and good news
- Celebrate meeting goals

Encourage friendships

- Suggest joining employee social groups and/or clubs
- Suggest joining professional associations and networking groups

Plan fun activities, outings, and breaks

- Celebrate birthdays, work anniversaries, or holidays
- Create contests and challenges
- Volunteer for a local charity during a workday

Do You Distinguish Yourself as a Communicator?

Here are seven steps many managers overlook, but ones you should keep in mind:

1. Know your people. How do you stay in touch with them? Do you talk to them individually to understand what their challenges are, what they worry about, what questions they have, and what rumors are circulating, if any?

2. Make organizational information relevant. When you discuss the company's strategy and tactics, in person or in writing, do you clarify to employees how your points are relevant to what they do every day?

3. Find the root of a problem. When communicating about a problem, do you go beyond focusing on the immediate issue to look at what caused it?

4. Craft compelling arguments. Do you go overboard by explaining in abundant detail why something is a problem without focusing on actions and solutions?

5. Communicate with a collaborative style. Do you seek to build relationships and help others across the organization, sometimes when it's not related to delivering results?

6. Show empathy. Do you listen when a direct report is experiencing a problem? Or is your "go-to" to analyze the problem and overlook the individual who is affected by it?

7. Communicate as if you care. Do you offer praise and compliment people for a job well done? Do you champion team successes elsewhere in the organization?

Adapted from O'Quinn (2017).

The Collaboration Operating Platform

Operating Principles

- **Focus on team–not position:** Addresses the need to focus on results produced when all positions effectively interact on the business field.
- **Understand that everyone can play:** Recognizes that technology is the great enabler, allowing people everywhere to play and collaborate in business.
- **Embrace diversity:** Represents the prerequisite for partnering in global business and serves as a springboard for establishing trust. Diversity brings strength to teams.
- **Rely on one another:** Reinforces the team orientation and minimizes the silo mindset recognizing a "mutual" dependency between people and promoting genuine collaboration.
- **Promote both individual and team values:** Deals with managing values in a never-ending cycle to help ensure that the process for producing team results is working.
- **Seek skillful, adaptable players:** Promotes the need for flexibility for managing change; requires people and teams who can quickly assimilate and use new skills, information, and the like; and recognizes that multiple skills are needed to play the game of business.
- **Charge the team to perform the work:** Recognizes the self-directed nature of the team charged with performing the work and recognizes that the team's performance during the game (business) is left up to the team.
- **Empower players to win:** Speaks to the commitment to develop all employees so they are able to provide continuous feedback, all to help position people to make better decisions.
- **Coach teams to respond to changing conditions on their own:** Reinforces the application of a real team, self-directed, operating on a real-time basis responding to changing conditions.

- **Develop partners on the field:** Recognizes that all players on the business field are viewed as leaders and views every opportunity as a leadership development step.
- **Achieve cross-cultural agility:** Calls for leveraging relationships in business to achieve results and transcends technique in dealing with people across cultures.

Competencies

- **Communicativeness:** Effective performers recognize the essential value of continuous information exchange and the competitive advantage it brings. They actively seek information from a variety of sources and disseminate it in a variety of ways. They use modern technologies to access and circulate information, even across great distances. They take responsibility for ensuring that their people have the current and accurate information they need for success.
- **Problem solving and decision making:** Effective performers identify problems, solve them, act decisively, and show good judgment. They isolate causes from symptoms, and compile information and alternatives to illuminate problems or issues. They involve others as appropriate and gather information from a variety of sources. They find a balance between studying the problem and solving it. They readily commit to action and make decisions that reflect sound judgment.
- **Learning agility:** Effective performers continuously seek new knowledge. They are curious and want to know why. They learn quickly and use new information effectively. They create and foster a culture of interest, curiosity, and learning.
- **Customer orientation:** Effective performers stay close to customers and consumers. They view the organization through the eyes of the customer and go out of their way to anticipate and meet customer needs. They continually seek information and understanding regarding market trends.
- **Functional and technical expertise:** Effective performers are

knowledgeable and skilled in a functional specialty (such as finance, marketing, operations, information technologies, and human resources). They add organizational value through unique expertise in a functional specialty area. They remain current in their area of expertise and serve as a resource in that area for the organization.

- **Team player:** Effective performers are team oriented and identify with the larger organizational team and their role within it. They share resources, respond to requests from other parts of the organization, and support larger legitimate organizational agendas as more important than local or personal goals.

- **Sensitivity:** Effective performers value and respect the concerns and feelings of others. In the workplace, this compassion translates into behaviors that communicate empathy toward others, respect for the individual, and appreciation of diversity among team members.

- **Conflict management:** Effective performers recognize that conflict can be a valuable part of the decision-making process. They are comfortable with healthy conflict and support and manage differences of opinion. They thwart destructive competition or friction and use consensus and collaboration to debate and resolve issues.

- **Relationship building:** Effective performers understand that a primary factor in success is about establishing and maintaining productive relationships. They like interacting with people and are good at it. They devote appropriate time and energy to establishing and maintaining networks. They initiate contacts readily and maintain them over time. They are able to utilize relationships to facilitate business transactions.

- **Strategic thinking:** Effective performers act with the future in mind. They plan and make decisions within the framework of the enterprise's strategic intent. They know and understand the factors influencing strategy (such as core competence, customers, competition, and the organization's current strengths and limitations). They consider future impact when weighing decisions, and think in terms of expanding the business, always looking for new ways to grow and achieve competitive advantage.

- **Influence:** Effective performers are skilled at directing, persuading, and motivating others. They are able to flex their style to direct, collaborate, or empower, as the situation requires. They have established a personal power base built on mutual trust, fairness, and honesty.
- **Risk taking:** Effective performers have a history of and propensity for taking calculated chances to achieve goals. They find a balance between analysis and action. When they fail, they accept it, learn from it, and move on to the next challenge.
- **Change agility:** Effective performers are adaptable. They embrace change and modify their behavior when appropriate to achieve organizational objectives. They are effective in the face of ambiguity. They understand and use change management techniques to help ensure smooth transitions.
- **Organizing and planning:** Effective performers have strong organizing and planning skills that allow them to be highly productive and efficient. They manage their time wisely, and effectively prioritize multiple competing tasks. They plan, organize, and actively manage meetings for maximum productivity.
- **Team management:** Effective performers create and maintain functional work units. They understand the human dynamics of team formation and maintenance. They formulate team roles and actively recruit and select to build effective work groups. They develop and communicate clear team goals and roles, and provide the level of guidance and management appropriate to the circumstances. They reward team behavior and foster a team atmosphere in the workplace.
- **Talent development:** Effective performers keep a continual eye on the talent pool, monitoring the skills and needs of all

team members. They expand the skills of staff through training, coaching, and development activities related to current and future jobs. They evaluate and articulate present performance and future potential to create opportunities for better use of staff abilities. They identify developmental needs and assist individuals in developing plans to improve themselves. They stay proficient in appropriate talent management processes, including best practices for prospecting, recruiting, selection, orientation, and succession management.

- **Results orientation:** Effective performers maintain appropriate focus on outcomes and accomplishments. They are motivated by achievement and persist until the goal is reached. They convey a sense of urgency to make things happen. They respect the need to balance short- and long-term goals. They are driven by a need for closure.

- **Positive impact:** Effective performers make positive impressions on those around them. They are personable, self-confident, and generally likeable. They are optimistic and enthusiastic about what they do, and their excitement is contagious. They energize those around them.

- **Integrity:** Effective performers think and act ethically and honestly. They apply ethical standards of behavior to their daily work activities and take responsibility for their actions and foster a work environment where integrity is rewarded.

- **Initiative:** Effective performers are proactive and take action without being prompted. They don't want to be told what to do or when to do it. They see a need, take responsibility, and act on it. They make things happen.

- **Drive and energy:** Effective performers have a high level of energy and the motivation to sustain it over time. They are ambitious and passionate about their role in the organization. They have the stamina and endurance to handle the substantial workload present in today's organizations. They know that a healthy work-life balance is important to sustained energy. They are motivated to maintain a fast pace and continue to produce even in exhausting circumstances.

- **Composure:** Effective performers maintain emotional control, even under ambiguous or stressful circumstances. They demonstrate emotions appropriate to the situation and continue performing steadily and effectively.

Adapted from the Polaris Competency Model with permission from Organization Systems International.

Your Preference for Collaboration?

To determine if you're a collaborative manager, score the statements below using the following scoring scale:

5 = Always   4 = Mostly   3 = Often   2 = Occasionally

1 = Rarely   0 = Never

	Score
I like to involve and consult with my direct reports about how they can best do their jobs.	
I want to learn skills outside my immediate area of responsibility.	
I allow direct reports to work without my interference but encourage them to ask for help.	
I cultivate an environment where direct reports work best and most productively without pressure or threat of losing their jobs.	
When direct reports leave the company, I conduct an exit interview to ask for their views on the organization.	
I incentivize and praise direct reports for working hard and well.	
I seek out opinions of direct reports to increase their responsibilities.	
I offer training to direct reports to learn new skills.	
I prefer to be friendly with my direct reports.	
I encourage direct reports to discuss their concerns, worries, or suggestions with me or another manager.	
I inform direct reports on what the company's aims and targets are.	
I let direct reports know how the company is performing on a regular basis.	
I give direct reports opportunities to solve problems connected with their work.	
I tell my direct reports what is happening elsewhere in the organization.	
I like to have regular meetings with my direct reports to discuss how they can improve and develop.	
Total	

Scoring Key:

60-75 = Strongly Prefers Collaboration

45-59 = Generally Prefers Collaboration

16-44 = Generally Does Not Prefer Collaboration

0-15 = Strongly Does Not Prefer Collaboration

What Does Collaboration Look Like for You?

To determine whether your operating principles are aligned with collaboration's mindset, check the operating principle(s) that apply to you in your job.

Operating Principle	You
Focus on Team, Not Position	
Understand That Everybody Can Play	
Embrace Diversity	
Rely on One Another	
Promote Both Individual and Team Values	
Seek Skillful, Adaptable Players	
Charge the Team to Perform the Work	
Empower Players to Win	
Coach Teams to Respond to Changing Conditions on Their Own	
Develop Partners on the Field	
Achieve Cross-Cultural Agility	
Total	

Theory X—Theory Y

The following Theory X—Theory Y questionnaire was devised by Alan Chapman as a learning aid and broad indicator directly based on McGregor's X—Y Theory. To determine whether the situation and management style is X or Y, score each of the statements below:

5 = Always   4 = Mostly   3 = Often   2 = Occasionally
1 = Rarely   0 = Never

	Score
My boss asks me politely to do things, gives me reasons why, and invites suggestions.	
I am encouraged to learn skills outside my immediate area of responsibility.	
I am left to work without interference from my boss, but help is available if I want it.	
I am given credit and praise when I do good work or put in extra effort.	
People leaving the company are given an exit interview to share their views on the organization.	
I am incentivized to work hard and well.	
If I want extra responsibility my boss will find a way to give it to me.	
If I want extra training my boss will help me find how to get it or will arrange it for me.	
I call my boss and my boss's boss by their first names.	
My boss is available for me to discuss my concerns, worries, and suggestions.	
I know what the company's aims and targets are.	
I am told how the company plans to achieve its aims and targets.	
I am given an opportunity to solve problems connected with my work.	

My boss tells me what is happening in the organization.	
I have regular meetings with my boss to discuss how I can improve and develop.	
Total	

Scoring Key:

60-75 = Strong Theory Y Management (effective long and short term)

45-59 = Generally Theory Y Management

16-44 = Generally Theory X Management

0-15 = Strong Theory X Management

Rate Your Proficiency With the Collaboration Competencies

Rate yourself on how the following competencies apply to your job. First impressions are usually right—don't spend a lot of time agonizing over your response. See the Collaboration Operating Principles tool for brief descriptions of each competency.

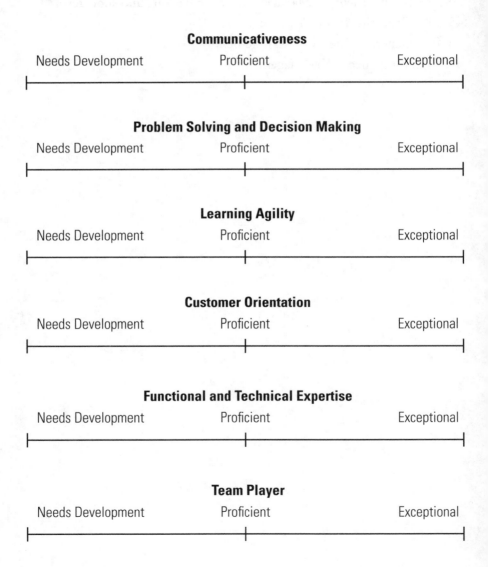

Communicativeness

Needs Development   Proficient   Exceptional

├─────────────────────────┼─────────────────────────┤

Problem Solving and Decision Making

Needs Development   Proficient   Exceptional

├─────────────────────────┼─────────────────────────┤

Learning Agility

Needs Development   Proficient   Exceptional

├─────────────────────────┼─────────────────────────┤

Customer Orientation

Needs Development   Proficient   Exceptional

├─────────────────────────┼─────────────────────────┤

Functional and Technical Expertise

Needs Development   Proficient   Exceptional

├─────────────────────────┼─────────────────────────┤

Team Player

Needs Development   Proficient   Exceptional

├─────────────────────────┼─────────────────────────┤

Sensitivity

Needs Development   Proficient   Exceptional

├─────────────────┼─────────────────┤

Conflict Management

Needs Development   Proficient   Exceptional

├─────────────────┼─────────────────┤

Relationship Building

Needs Development   Proficient   Exceptional

├─────────────────┼─────────────────┤

Strategic Thinking

Needs Development   Proficient   Exceptional

├─────────────────┼─────────────────┤

Influence

Needs Development   Proficient   Exceptional

├─────────────────┼─────────────────┤

Risk Taking

Needs Development   Proficient   Exceptional

├─────────────────┼─────────────────┤

Change Agility

Needs Development   Proficient   Exceptional

├─────────────────┼─────────────────┤

Organizing and Planning

Needs Development   Proficient   Exceptional

├─────────────────┼─────────────────┤

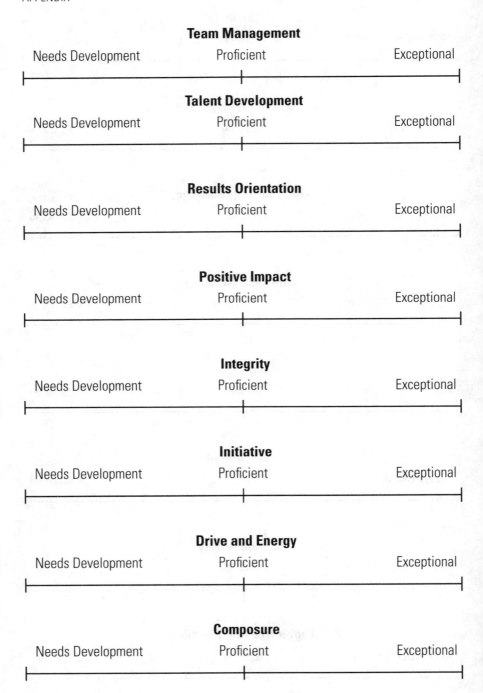

Team Management

Needs Development   Proficient   Exceptional

├──────────────────────────┼──────────────────────────┤

Talent Development

Needs Development   Proficient   Exceptional

├──────────────────────────┼──────────────────────────┤

Results Orientation

Needs Development   Proficient   Exceptional

├──────────────────────────┼──────────────────────────┤

Positive Impact

Needs Development   Proficient   Exceptional

├──────────────────────────┼──────────────────────────┤

Integrity

Needs Development   Proficient   Exceptional

├──────────────────────────┼──────────────────────────┤

Initiative

Needs Development   Proficient   Exceptional

├──────────────────────────┼──────────────────────────┤

Drive and Energy

Needs Development   Proficient   Exceptional

├──────────────────────────┼──────────────────────────┤

Composure

Needs Development   Proficient   Exceptional

├──────────────────────────┼──────────────────────────┤

Manager Engagement Worksheet

Create and Sustain Supportive Relationships	Share Organizational Information	Help Employees Feel Valued Through Frequent Feedback
✓ Get to know each employee's strengths, values, and motivators ✓ Ask employees what support they need to be successful ✓ Encourage questions and suggestions ✓ Support employee development and career growth How am I creating and sustaining supportive relationships with my employees?	✓ Help employees regularly reconnect to the mission and vision and understand how their work contributes to organizational success ✓ Align daily tasks with strategic goals ✓ Communicate key company information ✓ Share stories about positive customer results and emphasize how employees contributed to these results In what ways am I sharing organizational information with my team?	✓ Remember, everyone wants to be valued and respected ✓ Learn how your employees want to be recognized ✓ Acknowledge efforts and progress toward goals ✓ Remember, what gets recognized, gets repeated How am I providing regular feedback?
Hold Regular One-on-One Meetings	**Use a Coaching Approach to Improve Performance**	**Involve Employees**
✓ Provide an opportunity for employees to ask for support ✓ Ask employees to schedule the meetings ✓ Avoid canceling one-on-one meetings How am I regularly connecting with each of my team members?	✓ Plan ahead for positive, productive conversations ✓ Share your positive intent ✓ Make feedback for improvement future focused In what ways am I using a coaching approach to improve employee performance?	✓ Maximize opportunities for employees to add value ✓ Encourage employees to provide input and innovate ✓ Help employee learn about organizational realities How am I involving team members in driving our success?

Listening and Assessment Styles and Habits Self-Assessment

Let's see what kind of listener you are and how well you assess situations. This exercise captures your self-assessment but doesn't speak to how others perceive you. You can ask those close to you to complete the first three questions of the survey with you in mind; this will give you others' input on these same points.

1. If you had to characterize what kind of listener you are most of the time, please choose one or more of the following options that best describes your listening habits:
    - **Attentive listener.** I am a consistently good listener who is able to stay present and fully focused on what the other person is saying.
    - **Intermittent listener.** When I listen, I am a good listener; however, I also tend to get distracted, and in those moments, my listening skills aren't as good as they could be.
    - **Distracted listener.** I am frequently distracted by what I'm thinking or worried about distractions in the external environment, which in turn causes me not to be a particularly good listener.
    - **Poor listener.** As much as I endeavor to be a good listener, I find that listening is not my strong suit.
    - **Selective listener.** I often find that I am listening for the point I am trying to speak to or refute, tuning out the rest of what is being said.
    - **Opportunistic listener.** I usually find that I tune in to the things I want to hear and tune out those things I don't want to hear.
    - **Biased listener.** I find I often listen for those points the other person is saying that I agree with or disagree with at the expense of listening well, irrespective of agreement or lack thereof with what is being said.

- **Deficit-based listener.** I listen for gaps or inaccuracies in what someone is saying.
- **Convergent listener.** I listen for points the other person is making that I agree with, and tend not to focus on points of divergence.
- **Divergent listener.** I listen for points the other person is making that I disagree with, and tend not to focus on points of convergence.

2. Do you consider yourself to be a good listener?
   - Yes
   - No
   - Some of the time
   - Most of the time
   - Neutral

3. If you had to rank your top three bad listening habits, what would they be?
   - I will often find myself interrupting others, either out of impatience or because I am eager to assert my own opinion.
   - I regularly have the urge to finish or actually do finish others' sentences either out of impatience or an eagerness to agree or demonstrate my knowledge of what's being discussed.
   - I don't really listen; I am often distracted and am not adequately attending to what the other person is saying.
   - I think about what I am going to say in response versus fully listening to what they are saying.
   - I listen just enough to be able to assert my own point or counterpoint to what the other person is saying.
   - I focus more on my assessment of what the other person is saying than on what they are actually saying. I find it difficult to resist the urge to move to an evaluation of what the other person is saying instead of fully listening and then forming an opinion or response.

- I assert my voice or opinions without really listening to what the other person is saying.
- I make a judgment about what the other person is saying prematurely, thus tuning out before they make their point.
- I lose interest in what the other person is saying and then tune out.

4. Please choose your top three fears as they relate to your interactions with others:
   - I have a fear of being judged.
   - I have a fear of being misunderstood.
   - I have a fear of being wrong.
   - I have a fear of being viewed as unintelligent.
   - I have a fear of being perceived as uninformed.
   - I have a fear of being perceived as unknowledgeable.
   - I have a fear of being caught off guard.
   - I have a fear of not being able to contribute or make known my point of view.
   - I have a fear I will be called upon to contribute my point of view on a topic.
   - I have a fear that I won't get my way.
   - I have a fear that I will come off as being arrogant.
   - I have a fear that I will be perceived as too dramatic.
   - I have a fear of not being liked.
   - I have a fear of being too controversial.
   - I have a fear of not connecting with others.
   - I have a fear of not being accepted by others.
   - I have a fear of not fitting in.
   - I have a fear of being rejected outright.

5. Please rank, in order, how you most want to be seen or remembered by others:
   - It matters to me to be seen as someone who is knowledgeable.
   - It matters to me to be seen as someone who is intelligent.

- It matters to me to be seen as someone who is informed.
- It matters to me to be seen as someone who is nimble and capable of pivoting quickly.
- It matters to me to be seen as someone who is a subject matter expert.
- It matters to me to be seen as someone whose views are compelling or inspiring in some way.
- It matters to me to be seen as a good colleague, parent, partner, or friend.
- It matters to me whether I hurt someone else's feelings.
- It matters to me whether others view me as a good person.
- It matters to me whether others see me as a strong leader, one that others want to follow.
- It matters to me that I reach my personal or professional goals or objectives.
- It matters to me that I am perceived as someone who puts forth their best effort.
- It matters to me that others perceive me as resilient.
- It matters to me that others perceive me as caring and kind.
- It matters to me that others perceive me as an independent thinker.
- I want to be remembered as someone who questions the status quo.
- I want to be known as someone who chooses their words carefully and speaks succinctly.
- It matters to me that I act from my values (my moral compass).
- I want to be remembered as someone who sticks up for others.
- It matters to me that others are pushed a little out of their comfort zone or current boundaries of thought or opinion.

Acknowledgments

We have some serious kudos to dish out to everyone who helped make this book possible. First, we're indebted to the five experts and authorities who contributed chapters: Timothy Ito, Ken O'Quinn, Winsor Jenkins, Hunter Haines, and Michele Nevarez. You graciously poured your time, attention, and effort into making each of your chapters unique and thought provoking. You took our feedback in stride, and the book and our readers are better off for that.

Next, we want to thank the company we work for, the Association for Talent Development. Being part of a team oriented around creating a world that works better encourages and empowers us to take on a project like this one. The three of us brought different perspectives (Ryan content, Megan research, Jack editorial), and it's so cool that ATD enabled us to meld our experiences into this book. Specifically, we want to thank Maria Ho for her work on launching the research and developing the initial ACCEL model; Melissa Jones for guiding the book through copy editing and production; and Caroline Coppel for catching any last-minute errors with her proofreading.

References

Chapter 1

Branson, R. 2014. "You Learn by Doing and By Falling Over." Virgin Group, October 27. www.virgin.com/richard-branson/you-learn-by-doing-and-by-falling-over.

Comaford, C. 2016. "75% of Workers Are Affected By Bullying—Here's What to Do About It." *Forbes,* August 27. www.forbes.com/sites/christinecomaford/2016/08/27 /the-enormous-toll-workplace-bullying-takes-on-your-bottom-line/#1025cc475595.

Drucker, P. 2009. "Drucker on Management: The Five Deadly Business Sins." *Wall Street Journal,* November 18. First published October 21, 1993. www.wsj.com/articles /SB10001424052748704204304574544283192325934.

Harwell, D. 2017. "Hundreds Allege Sex Harassment, Discrimination at Kay and Jared Jewelry Company." *The Washington Post,* February 27. www.washingtonpost.com /business/economy/hundreds-allege-sex-harassment-discrimination-at-kay-and-jared -jewelry-company/2017/02/27/8dcc9574-f6b7-11e6-bf01-d47f8cf9b643_story.html ?utm_term=.cd76644fdba1.

Keller, T. 2013. "Chef Thomas Keller: Bouncing Back From Setbacks." Filmed April 15 at Stanford Graduate School of Business. Video, 59:04. www.youtube.com/watch?v =-8yFqrynkXE.

Lehrer, J. 2011. "Steve Jobs: 'Technology Alone Is Not Enough.'" *The New Yorker,* October 7. www.newyorker.com/news/news-desk/steve-jobs-technology-alone-is-not-enough.

Mankins, M., and E. Garton. 2017. "How Spotify Balances Employee Autonomy and Accountability." *Harvard Business Review,* February 9. https://hbr.org/2017/02/how -spotify-balances-employee-autonomy-and-accountability.

Mishel, L., E. Gould, and J. Bivens. 2015. "Wage Stagnation in Nine Charts." Economic Policy Institute, January 6. www.epi.org/publication/charting-wage-stagnation.

Partners in Leadership. 2014. "Accountability: The Low-Hanging Fruit for Optimizing Individual and Organizational Performance." *2014 Workplace Accountability Study.* https://info.partnersinleadership.com/workplace-accountability-study-executive -summary-download.

Saad, L. 2014. "The '40-Hour' Workweek Is Actually Longer—by Seven Hours." Gallup, August 29. https://news.gallup.com/poll/175286/hour-workweek-actually-longer-seven-hours.aspx

Steigrad, A. 2018. "Spotify Subscriber Count Reaches 83 Million." *New York Post,* July 26. https://nypost.com/2018/07/26/spotify-subscriber-count-reaches-83-million.

Steinberg, S.A., and E. Gurwitz. 2014. "The Underuse of Apprenticeships in America." Center for American Progress, July 22. www.americanprogress.org/issues/economy /news/2014/07/22/93932/the-underuse-of-apprenticeships-in-america.

Tobak, S. 2011. "Facebook's Mark Zuckerberg—Insights for Entrepreneurs." *CBS Money Watch,* October 31. www.cbsnews.com/news/facebooks-mark-zuckerberg-insights -for-entrepreneurs.

Whaples, R. 2001. "Hours of Work in U.S. History." EH.Net Encyclopedia, August 14. http://eh.net/encyclopedia/hours-of-work-in-u-s-history.

Whitbourne, S.K. 2012. "It's a Fine Line Between Narcissism and Egocentrism." *Psychology Today,* April 7. www.psychologytoday.com/us/blog/fulfillment-any-age/201204 /it-s-fine-line-between-narcissism-and-egocentrism.

Chapter 2

Bandura, A. 1990. "Conclusion: Reflections on Non-Ability Determinants of Competence." In *Competence Considered,* edited by R. Sternberg and J. Kolligian, 315-362. New Haven, CT: Yale University Press.

Barker, L.L., and K.W. Watson. 2000. *Listen Up: How to Improve Relationships, Reduce Stress, and Be More Productive by Using the Power of Listening.* New York: St. Martin's Press.

Blake, F. 2018. Interview with the author. March 19.

Brown, J.D. 1991. "Accuracy and Bias in Self-Knowledge." In *Handbook of Social and Clinical Psychology: The Health Perspective,* Pergamon General Psychology Series, vol. 162, edited by C.R. Snyder and D.R. Forsyth, 158-178. Elmsford, NY: Pergamon Press.

Carroll, J. 2010. Personal email to the author. September 11.

Case, J. 2018. Personal email to the author. January 13.

Collins, S. 2009. *Interpersonal Communication: Listening and Responding.* Module 5 in Managerial Communication, edited by J.S. O'Rourke. Mason, OH: South-Western Cengage Learning.

Doble, M. 2018. Personal interview with the author. February 16.

Drucker, P. 1954. *The Practice of Management.* New York: Harper Business.

Fugere, B., C. Hardaway, and J. Warshawsky. 2005. *Why Business People Speak Like Idiots: A Bullfighter's Guide.* New York: Free Press.

Goldhaber, G.M. 1984. *Information Strategies: New Pathways to Management Productivity.* New York: Ablex Publishing.

Gratton, L. 2008. "Counterpoint: Lynda Gratton." *People + Strategy,* September 1. www.thefreelibrary.com/Counterpoint%3A+Lynda+Gratton.-a0200784489.

Hodding, C. 2018. Personal interview with the author. February 9.

Jones, E.E., and R.E. Nisbett. 1987. "The Actor and the Observer: Divergent Perceptions of the Causes of Behavior." In *Attribution: Perceiving the Causes of Behavior,* edited by E.E. Jones, D.E. Kanouse, H.H. Kelley, R.E. Nisbett, S. Valins, and B. Weiner, 79-94. Hillsdale, NJ: Lawrence Erlbaum Associates.

Knowles, E.S., and J.A. Linn. 2004. "Approach-Avoidance Model of Persuasion: Alpha and Omega Strategies for Change." In *Resistance and Persuasion,* edited by E.S. Knowles and J.A. Linn, 117-148. Mahwah, NJ: Lawrence Erlbaum Associates.

Kotter, J. 1995. "Leading Change: Why Transformation Efforts Fail." *Harvard Business Review,* May-June. https://hbr.org/1995/05/leading-change-why-transformation-efforts-fail-2.

Locke, E., and G.P. Latham. 1990. *A Theory of Goal Setting and Task Performance.* New York: Pearson.

Miller, D., and M. Ross. 1975. "Self-Serving Biases in Attribution of Causality: Fact or Fiction?" *Psychological Bulletin* 82: 213-225.

Nichols, R., and L. Stevens. 1957. "Listening to People." *Harvard Business Review,* September.

O'Keefe, D. 2002. *Persuasion: Theory & Research.* Thousand Oaks, CA: Sage.

O'Quinn, K. 2017. "Business Writing for Managers." *TD at Work.* Alexandria, VA: ATD Press.

Ryan, P. 2018. Personal interview with the author. March.

Samson, D. 2018. Personal interview with the author. March 14.

Sinickas, A. 2018. Personal interview with the author. February 7.

Staw, B., L. Sandelands, and J. Dutton. 1981. "Threat-Rigidity Effects in Organizational Behavior." *Administrative Science Quarterly* 26(4): 501-524.

Stone, D., B. Patton, and S. Heen. 1999. *Difficult Conversations: How to Discuss What Matters Most.* New York: Bantam Doubleday Dell.

Sullivan, J. 2018. Personal email to author. January 2.

Tengblad, S. 2006. "Is There a New Managerial Work?" *Journal of Management Studies* 43(7): 1437-1461.

Thiry, K. 2018. Personal interview with author. March 25.

Tsiky, A. 2018. Personal email to author. January 8.

Weeks, H. 2010. *Failure to Communicate: How Conversations Go Wrong and What You Can Do to Right Them.* Boston: Harvard Business Review Press.

Weeks, H. 2018. Personal email to author. March 17.

Yates, K. 2018. Personal interview with author. January 10.

Chapter 3

Buckingham, M., and C. Coffman. 1999. *First Break All the Rules.* New York: Simon & Schuster.

Carlin, J. 2008. *Invictus: Nelson Mandela and the Game That Made a Nation.* New York: Penguin Books.

Covey, S.R. 2004. *The 8th Habit: From Effectiveness to Greatness.* New York: Free Press.

Dishman, L. 2016. "The One Skill That Impacts Overall Success." *Fast Company,* February 2. www.fastcompany.com/3056176/the-one-leadership-skill-that-impacts-overall-success.

Duhigg, C. 2016. "Group Study." *New York Times,* February 28.

Dweck, C. 2008. *Mindset: The New Psychology of Success.* New York: Ballentine Books.

Farson, R. 1996. *Management of the Absurd.* New York: Simon & Schuster.

Goleman, D. 1995. *Emotional Intelligence: Why It Can Matter More Than IQ.* New York: Bantam Books.

Goleman, D., R. Boyatis, and A. McKee. 2002. *Primal Leadership: Learning to Lead With Emotional Intelligence.* Boston: Harvard Business Press.

Griffiths, B., and E. Washington. 2015. *Competencies at Work.* Business Expert Press.

Hamel, G. 2006. "The Why, What, and How of Management Innovation." *Harvard Business Review,* February.

IBM. 2012. *Leading Through Connections: Insights From the Global Chief Executive Officer Study.* CEO C-Suite Studies. New York: IBM Institute for Business Value. www-935.ibm.com/services/multimedia/ anz_ceo_study_2012.pdf.

IBM. 2013. *The Customer-Activated Enterprise: Insights From the Global C-Suite Study.* New York: IBM Institute for Business Value. www-01.ibm.com/common/ssi/cgi-bin /ssialias?htmlfid=GBE03572USEN.

Jenkins, W. 1997a. "Situational Leadership." *The Soccer Journal.*

Jenkins, W. 1997b. "Soccer Metaphor Works Best." *The Soccer Journal.*

Jenkins, W. 1998. "Partners on the Field." *The Soccer Journal.*

Jenkins, W. 2005. "Perspective: The Pitch for a New Leadership Metaphor." *The Journal of The Human Resources Planning Society.*

Jenkins, W. 2007. *The Collaborator: Discover Soccer as a Metaphor for Global Business Leadership.* Lake Oswego, OR: DW Publishing.

Katzenbach, J., and D. Smith. 1994. *The Wisdom of Teams.* New York: Harper Business.

McGregor, D. 1960. *The Human Side of Enterprise.* New York: McGraw-Hill

McGregor, D. n.d. "McGregor XY Theory of Management." Businessballs.com. www.business balls.com/improve-workplace-performance/mcgregors-xy-theory-of-management-4042.

McIntosh, P. 1968. *Physical Education in England Since 1800.* London: G. Bell and Sons, LTD.

Peters, J., and C. Carr. 2013. *High Performance Team Coaching: A Comprehensive System for Leaders and Coaches.* Victoria, BC: Friesen Press.

Petrie, N. 2015. "Future Trends in Leadership Development." Whitepaper. Center for Creative Leadership. www.ccl.org/wp-content/uploads/2015/04/futureTrends.pdf.

Rosen, E. 2007. *The Culture of Collaboration: Maximizing Time, Talent, and Tools to Create Value in the Global Economy.* San Francisco, CA: Red Ape Publishing.

Schein, E. 2010. *Organizational Culture and Leadership.* Hoboken, NJ: John Wiley and Sons.

Shook, J. 2010. "How to Change a Culture: Lessons From NUMMI." Research Feature. *MIT Sloan Management Review,* January 1. www.sloanreview.mit.edu/article/how-to -change-a-culture-lessons-rfom-nummi.

Urch Drusak, V., and S. Wolff. 2001. "Building the Emotional Intelligence of Groups." *Harvard Business Review,* March.

Zohar, D. 2009. "An Alternative Sports Metaphor for Understanding Teamwork as Complex: Soccer." *Emergence: Complexity and Organization,* June 30. https://journal.emergentpublica-tions.com/article/an-alternative-sports-metaphor-for-understanding-teamwork-as-complex.

Chapter 4

Airbnb. 2015. "Employee Experience Department." May 13. www.airbnb.com/careers /departments/employee-experience.

Gallup. 2015. "The State of the American Manager: Analytics and Advice for Leaders." April 2. www.gallup.com/services/182216/state-american-manager-report.aspx).

Gallup. 2018. "Gallup Daily: U.S. Employee Engagement." February 10. http://news .gallup.com/poll/180404/gallup-daily-employee-engagement.aspx.

Garvin, D.A. 2013. "How Google Sold Its Engineers on Management." *Harvard Business Review,* December: 74–82.

Gibbons, J. 2006. *Employee Engagement: A Review of Current Research and Its Implications.* New York: The Conference Board.

Kahn, W.A. 1990. "Psychological Conditions of Personal Engagement and Disengagement at Work." *Academy of Management Journal* 33(4): 692-724.

Kouzes, J.M., and B.Z. Posner. 2011. *Credibility: How Leaders Gain and Lose It, Why People Demand It.* 2nd Ed. San Francisco: Jossey-Bass.

Lencioni, P. 2002. *The Five Dysfunctions of a Team.* San Francisco: Jossey-Bass.

Robinson, D., S. Perryman, and S. Hayday. 2004. *The Drivers of Employee Engagement.* Brighton, UK: Institute for Employment Studies.

SHRM (Society for Human Resource Management). 2017. "Developing and Sustaining Employee Engagement." May 17. www.shrm.org/resourcesandtools/tools-and-samples /toolkits/pages/sustainingemployeeengagement.aspx.

Swindall, C. 2007. *Engaged Leadership: Building a Culture to Overcome Employee Disengagement.* Hoboken, NJ: John Wiley and Sons.

Towers Perrin. 2003. "Working Today: Understanding What Drives Employee Engagement."

Chapter 5

ABC Science. 2012. "Is There Such a Thing as a Super Hearer?" Ask an Expert, July 25. www.abc.net.au/science/articles/2012/07/25/3553426.htm.

Center for Healthy Minds. 2016. "Changing Your Brain and Generosity Through Compassion Meditation Training." University of Wisconsin-Madison. https://centerhealthyminds.org/ science/studies/changing-your-brain-and-generosity-through-compassion-meditation-training.

Finlay, L. 2015. *Relational Integrative Psychotherapy: Engaging Process and Theory in Practice.* Malden, MA: Wiley. http://relational-integrative-psychotherapy.uk/chapters /empathising-and-attuning.

Greenberg, L.S., L.N. Rice, and R. Elliott. 1993. *Facilitating Emotional Change: The Moment-by-Moment Process.* New York: Guilford Press.

Lutz, A., J. Brefczynski-Lewis, T. Johnstone, and R.J. Davidson. 2008. "Regulation of the Neural Circuitry of Emotion by Compassion Meditation: Effects of Meditative Expertise." *PLOS One,* March 26. https://journals.plos.org/plosone/article?id=10.1371 /journal.pone.0001897.

Mlodinow, L. 2012. *Subliminal: How Your Unconscious Mind Rules Your Behavior.* New York: Random House.

Nawaz, S. 2018. "How to Create Executive Team Norms—and Make Them Stick." *Harvard Business Review,* January 15. https://hbr.org/2018/01/how-to-create-executive-team-norms-and-make-them-stick.

About the Contributors

Hunter Haines

Hunter Haines, MS, ACC, CPLP, ODCP, is a senior organization development and inclusion consultant at the University of Maryland Medical System and president of People Leading People, a company that provides leadership and team coaching. Hunter is known for her compassionate and results-oriented approach to helping leaders and teams achieve exceptional results. She challenges leaders to be intentional about their leadership practice and to maximize their impact on individual, team, and organizational performance.

Hunter has worked with (and learned from) leaders and teams at organizations including Exelon, CareFirst BlueCross BlueShield, and Johns Hopkins University. She is a mentor coach for the Maryland University of Integrative Health and a Certified Marshall Goldsmith Stakeholder Centered Coach. Hunter graduated from Johns Hopkins University with a BS in business, an MS in applied behavioral science, and a graduate certificate in change management.

Hunter holds the Certified Professional in Learning and Performance (CPLP) certification from the Association of Talent Development (ATD) and is a past-president of ATD Maryland. She is an Associate Certified Coach and member of the International Coach Federation (ICF). She supports both ATD and ICF in promoting the professional talent development and coaching communities in Maryland, where she lives with her family. Hunter can be reached at hunter@peopleleadingpeople.com.

Timothy Ito

Timothy Ito is currently a vice president at the Association for Talent Development, overseeing the content and digital marketing division of the organization. Previous to ATD, he ran the content marketing group for ASCD, including oversight of the business and revenue strategy for ASCD's digital properties (website, video content, mobile applications, and e-commerce). Tim's career has also included stints at America Online and Netscape as the product and strategy lead for AOL e-commerce in careers and real estate, and running the business operations for Netscape Japan and the Netscape International channels.

Tim is a former senior editor and producer at AltaVista and washingtonpost.com, and was a reporter and writer for *U.S. News & World Report* magazine. He began his professional career teaching English at a Japanese High School in Tokyo, Japan.

Winsor Jenkins

Winsor Jenkins is president of Winsor Jenkins & Associates, which is based in Portland, Oregon. His company specializes in talent development, including coaching.

Winsor has spent more than 30 years with three publicly traded companies, which has given him the knowledge, insights, and tools to help people and organizations achieve results. As a leader who served in senior human resources positions (including vice president) and contributed to the professional development of business executives at all levels, he brings a deep understanding of what it takes to lead in today's changing global business world.

Along with holding coaching certifications from the Hudson Institute of Coaching and the International Coach Federation, Winsor is a certified facilitator in several best-in-class leadership development training programs including Situational Leadership II, as well as various assessments used in training and coaching such as MBTI and Polaris 360. He has a bachelor of science from Cornell University and an MBA from the University of Idaho.

Winsor is the author of *The Collaborator: Discover Soccer as a Metaphor for Global Business* and also serves as co-designer of the training program The Collaboration Game. He has written articles for the *Soccer Journal* and *The Journal of The Human Resources Planning Society*, along with writing blog posts for the Association for Talent Development.

Michele Nevarez

Michele Nevarez, an executive coach and seasoned HR executive, heads up the Daniel Goleman Emotional Intelligence Coaching and Training programs. Leveraging emotional intelligence, she helps leaders tap into their self-efficacy by developing self-awareness, focus, and resilience. She is also an adjunct faculty member for Cultivating Well Being in the Workplace: A Neuroscientific Approach, a program co-developed by the University of Wisconsin-Madison School of Business and the Center for Healthy Minds. Michele brings more than 20 years of HR leadership and C-suite experience working for industry leaders in healthcare, manufacturing, investment management, and management consulting.

Ken O'Quinn

Ken O'Quinn is a communications workshop leader, a corporate writing expert, and an author and speaker for ATD. His professional business writing and management communication workshops have helped thousands of business professionals around the globe improve their communication skills.

He started Writing with Clarity following a journalism career with the Associated Press and now conducts workshops for corporations throughout the world. He is the author of *Perfect Phrases for Business Letters* (McGraw-Hill) and *Business Writing for Managers* (ATD Press). His clients include Facebook, GE, Chevron, Dell, KPMG, Cisco, Campbell's Soup, Oracle, the Gap, SAP (worldwide), Dow Chemical (China), Fidelity Investments, Northrop Grumman, Raytheon, and Reebok.

Ken speaks at many business conferences, and his writing has appeared in *Fast Company* magazine, the *New York Times,* the *Harvard Management Communication Letter,* and the *Journal of Employee Communication Management.*

About the Editors

Ryan Changcoco

Ryan Changcoco is an author, blogger, thought leader, and facilitator on the topics of management development and employee engagement. As the senior manager for ATD's management development and TD industries group, Ryan is responsible for identifying and partnering with subject matter experts from all over the world to develop content in the areas of management development, leadership, and industries training. Ryan is also the program director for the ATD/Yale Management Excellence program. Prior to ATD, Ryan served as a business consultant for several large healthcare organizations, including Blue Cross and Blue Shield. Ryan is also the co-founder of a physician advisory and consulting group called The Physician's Edge, which is dedicated to helping physicians become more adept at the business side of healthcare.

As an author, Ryan has contributed to a few healthcare publications including *Talent Management in Healthcare—Exploring How the World's Health Service Organisations Attract, Manage and Develop Talent* (2017) and *Leadership in the World's Healthcare Sector* (2018), both of which were published by Palgrave Macmillan UK.

When asked what three phrases best describe him, Ryan's response is: optimist, traveler, and free spirit.

Megan Cole

Megan Cole, PhD, is a research analyst at the Association for Talent Development (ATD). She regularly writes research reports, blogs, and magazine articles, as well as hosting webcasts. She has authored numerous research reports on talent development topics including *The Science of Learning: Key Strategies for Designing and Delivering Training, Needs Assessments: Design and Execution for Success,* and *Change Enablement: Skills for Addressing Change.*

One of her first projects at ATD was creating research around the ACCEL model—published as *ACCEL: The Skills That Make a Winning Manager*—that eventually led to the creation of *Focus on Them.* Megan has since been involved in the development of other ACCEL-related content.

Megan has also worked as a market research analyst and an instructor at Arizona State University. She has published articles in several peer-reviewed journals, including *Journal of Computer-Mediated Communication, Journal of Nonverbal Behavior,* and most recently *Journal of Social Psychology.* Her work has been featured in *Time, Forbes, Huffington Post, PBS News Hour,* and *US News & World Report.*

Megan received bachelor's and master's degrees from the University of Central Florida. She earned a doctorate in communication from Arizona State University.

Jack Harlow

Jack Harlow has spent his entire career managing people—writers, that is. As a developmental editor with the Association for Talent Development, Jack works behind the scenes with notable subject matter experts—such as Clark Quinn, Karl M. Kapp, and the *Focus on Them* contributors—to develop book concepts that resonate with readers.

Just like managing direct reports, Jack's role empowers him to apply ATD's ACCEL model: He applies a human-centered culture of accountability with authors and other stakeholders. He leverages his experience with language to communicate clearly and build trust. He adopts a collaborative mindset to coach authors through the publication process. He applies the latest findings around workplace apathy to engage authors. And finally, he listens to authors because their stories are the ones worth telling and he wants to see them all shine.

Before joining ATD, Jack served as an editor for Communications Development Incorporated, an editorial and design house in Washington, D.C. There he filled a jack-of-all-trades role as proofreader, copy editor, content developer, and project manager on economic and development reports for the World Bank and United Nations organizations.

Based in Alexandria, Virginia, Jack lives with his wife, Casey, and three pets Obi-Wan, Wookiee, and Barney. He has a masters in publishing from George Washington University's College of Professional Studies and a bachelors in English language and literature from the University of Maryland.

Index

A

ABC Science, 119
ACCEL: The Skills That Make a Winning Manager (Association for Talent Development), x, 67, 101
ACCEL skills model of management
  accountability, xii
  collaboration, xii–xiii
  communication, xi–xii
  engagement, xiii
  listening and assessing, xiii–xiv
  polling regarding, x
accidental managers, ix
accountability. *See also* FACES approach to accountability
  demands from investors and employees, 32–33
  introduction, xi
  perceptions regarding, xi, 2
  for poor managerial performance, 101
  team, 2
  Thomas Keller example of developing employees, 24–25
  vs. productivity, 7, 8–9
Airbnb example of improving engagement, 98–99
alignment, 6
alignment of purpose, 133–135
amygdala and managing emotions, 140–142, 145
apprenticeship, 7–9
Aristotle, 37
article rewriting example of meaningless challenges, 12–13

assumptions, underlying, 73–75
attitude and behavior, 105–108, 110
audiences
  analyzing, 37
  complacent, 38–39
  resistant, 38
  supportive, 38
authenticity, 35–36

B

Bandura, Albert, 47
Barker, Larry, 52
Barsoux, Jean-Louis, 54
Ben example of mindfulness in a meeting, 128–129
Bennis, Warren, 73
Berlo, David, 30
bias
  actor-observer, 45–46
  confirmation, 120–121, 136
  self-serving, 46
  unconscious, 136–137, 146
Blake, Frank, 34
Blanchard, Ken, 110
brain training for intrapersonal listening skills, 139–142
Branson, Richard, 21
Buckingham, Marcus, 78

C

caring, demonstrating, 33–35
Carnegie, Dale, 29

Carr, Catherine, 90
Carter, Hodding, 35–36
Case, John, 32
case studies
    Erick and Dan (apprenticeship approach), 7–8
    Erin and Brad (email communication), 49–50
    hypothetical manager (collaboration operating platform), 81–84
    Lauren (self-awareness), 125–126
    Robin (collaborative team coach), 84–85
    Spotify (balancing creativity with accountability), 6
    Tim and Kurt (collaborative team manager), 70–71
    Toni (global collaboration), 64
    U.S. News & World Report fact-checking department, 1–2, 5, 7–8, 14
challenges
    achievable, 10–11
    article rewriting example of meaningless, 12–13
    long-term *vs.* short-term, 11–12
    meaningful, 12–13
    setting deadlines for, 11
    video game example of achievable, 10
change
    telegraphing, 19–20
    website redesign example of telegraphing, 20
Chapman, Alan, 164–165
coaching
    advantages of, 85
    approach to giving feedback, 109–113
    a collaborative team manager, 70
    to develop a collaborative team mindset, 87–88
    to improve interpersonal listening skills, 143
    responsibilities, 85–86
    Robin (collaborative team coach) case study, 84–85
Coffman, Curt, 78
cognitive dissonance, 41
collaboration
    coaching a collaborative team manager, 70–71
    creating an environment of teamwork, xii–xiii, 67, 68
    delegation, 77–78
    developing self-awareness, 71–73, 90, 125–126, 142, 144
    genuine, 62–63, 91
    introduction, xi–xiii
    as the key to organizational success, 65–66
    mindset, 69–70, 163
    operating platform, applying the, 81–84

operating principles and competencies, 69–70, 75–77, 86–87, 153–158, 163, 164–166
    preferences survey (Appendix), 159–160
    psychological safety as a necessity for teamwork, 67, 90
    skill set, 69–70, 76–77
    soccer analogy, 66
    team mini-charter for developing a culture of, 86–87
    team norms, 89–90, 135–136, 137–138
    Toni (global collaboration) case study, 64
    in the VUCA world, 67
    win-win scenarios, 61–62
The Collaborator (Jenkins), 62, 66
commitment, 41
communication. *See also* feedback
    clarity, 45
    developments timeline, 29–31
    difficult conversations, 44–46
    early communication to telegraph change, 19–20
    from effective managers, xii, 27–28, 59–60
    by email, 48–51
    Internet and social media, 30–31
    introduction, xi–xii
    language choice, 29, 60
    listening skills, 51–55, 117–118, 124–136, 139–147
    matching words with actions, 32–32
    miscommunication, xi–xii
    neutral tone, 45–46
    new methods of, xi–xii
    rhetoric, 28
    source-message-channel-receiver (SMCR) model, 30
    temperance, 4
compassion practice, 140–141
competencies, developing, 69–70, 75–76, 88–89
confirmation bias, 120–121, 136–137
conflict, managing team, 83, 86–87, 107
consistency, 41
Contaldi, Ellen, 17
context for understanding work expectations, 4
Covey, Steven R., 65
creativity
    harnessing, 5–6
    innovation, 15–16
credibility
    building, 31–32
    judging, 37
    and persuasion, 36–37

Csiky, Alan, 32
culture
   of collaboration, 86–87, 91–92
   team, 78–81
curiosity, 21
The Customer-Activated Enterprise (study), 67

D

Davidson, Richard, 140–141
day-to-day responsibilities, 4–7
delegation, 77–78
Difficult Conversations (Stone, Patton, and Heen), 45
Doble, Mike, 43, 51
dream jobs, 103–104
Drucker, Peter, 11, 28
Dweck, Carol, 88

E

Ed (Ryan Changcoco's former manager), vii–viii
education
   management's role in encouraging learning, 14–16
   value of broad learning experiences, 15–16
email communication, 48–51
emotional balance, 129–130
emotional intelligence (EQ), xiv, 71, 90–91
empathic attunement, 131–133
employee experience, improving the, 98–99
employee satisfaction *vs.* employee engagement, 95
"Empty your cup" metaphor for listening, 148
engagement. *See also* managers' effect on
      employee engagement
   Airbnb example of improving, 98–99
   defined, 95
   described, 95–96
   effect on organizational success, 93
   factors affecting, 98–99
   increasing employee, ix, xiii
   introduction, xiii
   manager worksheet (Appendix), 167
   mutual benefits of, 96
   psychological conditions that influence, 96–97
   Sharon example of engagement's effect on
      employee performance, 94
   uncontrollable factors affecting, 99
   vs. employee satisfaction, 95
Erick and Dan (apprenticeship approach)
   case study, 7–8
Erin and Brad (email communication) case
   study, 48–51

F

FACES approach to accountability. *See also*
      accountability
   about, 2–3
   accountability checklist (Appendix), 150
   apprenticeship, 7–9
   challenge, 9–14
   education, 14–16
   focus, 3–7
   and the long-term interests of employees,
      25–26
   performance management, 23–24
   safety, 16–24
Facilitating Emotional Change (Greenberg,
   Rice, and Elliot), 132
failure, 22, 36
Failure to Communicate (Weeks), 45–46
feedback. *See also* communication
   360, 143
   actionable, 43
   delivering, 44–55
   difficult conversations, 44–46
   by email, 48–51
   focusing on the behavior instead of the
      individual, 47–48
   frequency, 47
   guidelines, 111–113
   helping employees feel valued, 105–108
   holding regular one-on-one meetings,
      108–109
   inviting input by asking questions, 54
   listening skills, 51–54, 117–118, 124–136,
      139–147
   for managers, 42–43
   from multiple sources, 42–43
   positive, 105–108
   purpose of, 42–43
   "set-up to fail syndrome," 54–55
   specificity, 51
   using a coaching approach, 109–113
Festinger, Leon, 41
Finlay, Linda, 132
First Break All the Rules (Buckingham and
   Coffman), 78
The Five Dysfunctions of a Team (Lencioni), 107
focus, 3–7, 126–127
Fraser, Douglas, 30
Fugere, Brian, 39–40
fun environments, creating (Appendix), 151

G

Gallup Organization's Q-12, 78–81, 98
Garton, Eric, 6
Goleman, Daniel, 71
Gratton, Lynda, 43
Griffiths, Bruce, 67, 73, 76–78

H

Haines, Hunter, xiii, 94–95, 103–104, 111, 115
honesty and integrity, 35–36
How to Win Friends and Influence People
   (Carnegie), 29
The Human Side of Enterprise (McGregor), 74

I

influence, 137–138
innovation, 15–16
integrity and honesty, 35–36
intentions, setting, 141–142
Internet and social media, 30–31
interpersonal listening skills, 130–136, 142–144
intrapersonal listening skills, 124–130, 139–142
Ito, Timothy, xi, 1–3, 5, 12–14, 16

J

Jenkins, Winsor, xii–xiii, 61–62, 66, 80–81
Jobs, Steve, 15
Jordan-Evan, Sharon, 115

K

Kahn, William, 96–97
Kaye, Beverly, 115
Keller, Thomas, 24–25
Kellogg, Jon, 54
Kotter, John, 33

L

language
   creating a persuasive message, 39–42, 60
   overused terms, 39–40
   rhetoric, 28
Lauren (self-awareness) case study, 125–126
Leading Through Connections (study), 67
learning
   management's role in encouraging, 14–16
   value of diverse knowledge, 15–16
Lencioni, Patrick, 107

listening and assessing
   active listening, 131
   alignment of purpose, 133–135
   common pitfalls, 120–124
   confirmation bias, 120–121
   demonstrating tolerance for different
      perspectives, 138–139
   empathic attunement, 131–133
   "Empty your cup" metaphor, 148
   improving listening misbehavior, 124
   influence, 137–138
   interpersonal listening skills, 130–136, 142–144
   interrupting, 117
   intrapersonal listening skills, 124–130, 139–142
   introduction, xiii–xiv
   paying attention, 119–120
   processing sensory input, 119
   purpose of, xiii–xiv
   reflective listening, 130–131
   sensory improvement, 118–120
   social awareness, 133
   speaker and listener roles, 120–124
   strategies to get back on track, 144–147
   styles and habits self-assessment (Appendix),
      168–171
   unconscious bias, 136–137, 145
listening skills, 51–55, 117–118, 124–136, 139–147
Love 'Em or Lose 'Em (Kaye and Jordan-Evan), 115

M

management
   accidental managers, ix
   bad bosses, ix
   chain of command mindset, 65
   changing approaches to, vii, 27–28
   communication development timeline, 29–31
   employee oversight and time constraints, 5, 6
   flexibility, 73
   hostile managers, 18–19
   ineffective managers, 100
   leadership promotions as a retention strategy, 100
   role in encouraging learning, 14–16
   "set-up to fail syndrome," 54–55
   skills, 101
   starting your first managerial role, 64–65, 71–74
   styles, adjusting, 77–78
   systems, trendy, 28
   transparency, 31–32
   working managers, 100–101

managers' effect on employee engagement.
   See also engagement
   creating and sustaining supportive relationships, 102–104
   dynamics of listening, 135–139
   helping employees feel valued, 105–108
   holding regular one-on-one meetings, 108–109
   involving employees, 114–115
   manager engagement worksheet (Appendix), 167
   performance feedback, 109–113
   sharing organizational information, 104–105
Mandela, Nelson, 61–63
Mankin, Michael, 6
Manzoni, Jean-Francois, 54–55
McGregor, Douglas, 74–75
McIntosh, Peter, 66
meditation, 139–141
meetings
   Ben example of mindfulness in, 127–128
   controlling the discussion, 57–59
   creating an agenda and sticking to it, 57
   determining necessity, 56
   ending and following up on action items, 59
   inviting the relevant participants, 56–57
   one-on-one, 108–109
   opinions regarding, 54–55
mentoring, 114–115
mindfulness, 127–128
Mindset: The New Psychology of Success (Dweck), 88
mindset(s)
   chain of command, 65
   collaboration, 67–68, 82, 161
   compliance *vs.* commitment, 80–81
   fixed *vs.* growth, 880
   leading with a, 75–76
   silo, 88
   team, 87–88
Mlodinow, Leonard, 137
motivation
   to improve interpersonal listening skills, 142
   intrinsic, 2
   understanding, 72
mountain climbing analogy for assessing
      team culture, 78–79

N

narcissism, 18
Nevarez, Michele, xiv, 117–120, 129
Nichols, Ralph, 53

norms, team, 89–90, 135–136, 137–138
NUMMI example of Theory X and Theory Y
   assumptions, 74–75

O

The One Minute Manager (Blanchard and
   Spender), 110
Open Book Management, 32
O'Quinn, Ken, xii
organizational information, sharing, 104–105
Organization Culture and Leadership (Schein), 75
Our Senses: An Immersive Experience (exhibit), 119

P

Patterson, Alan, 7
performance, team, 85–86, 90
performance management, 23–24
persuasion
   analyzing the audience, 37–39
   asking for less initially, 41–42
   "bandwagon" effect, 40
   consistency and commitment, 41
   and credibility, 36–37
   imagining potential outcomes, 40
   and language choice, 39–40, 60
   as a science, 36
Peters, Jacqueline, 90
Phillips, Kathleen, 2–5, 14, 23
Physical Education in England Since 1800
   (McIntosh), 66
pivoting, 144–145
positivity, 22–23
prefrontal cortex (PFC) and managing emotions,
   140–141, 144
prioritization, 4–7
problem solving
   hypothetical manager (collaboration operating
      platform) case study, 81–83
productivity, 7–9, 115
promoting technical experts to management roles, 100
public relations scandals, 31–32

Q

Q-12, 78–81, 98

R

resilience, 140
respect, 105–108

risk, 20–22
Robin (collaborative team coach) case study, 84–85
rules for teams, 87–88

S

safety
    early communication, 19–20
    positivity, 22–23
    psychological, 67, 90
    risk, 20–22
    Sterling Jewelers example of a hostile work
        environment, 17–18
Samson, Dave, 27, 33, 35, 44
Schein, Edgar, 75, 86
self-awareness, developing, 71–73, 91, 125–126,
    142, 144
self-management, 129
silo mindset, 88
Sinickas, Angela, 34–35
skills
    interpersonal listening, 130–136, 142–144
    intrapersonal listening, 124–130, 139–142
    listening, 51–54, 117–118, 124–136, 139–147
    management, 101
soccer analogy of collaboration in global
    business, 66
social awareness, 133
Spender, Richard, 110
Spotify (balancing creativity with accountability)
    case study, 6
Stevens, Leonard, 53
stress, reacting to, 129
Sullivan, Jerome, 31
support, providing, 102–104

T

team culture, 78–80
team(s)
    dynamics of listening, 135–139
    EQ, 90–91
    mindset, 87–88
mini-charter for developing a culture of
    collaboration, 86–87
norms, 89–90, 135–136, 135–136
stages of performance, 85–86
Theory X and Theory Y, 74–75, 80–81, 162–163
Thiry, Kent, 33, 35
Thomas Keller example of developing
    employees, 24–25

thoughtfulness, demonstrating, 33–35
Tim and Kurt (collaborative team manager)
    case study, 70–71
time
    as a barrier to exhibiting ACCEL skills, 115
    deadlines for challenges, 11
    employee oversight and time constraints, 5, 6
    increases in work hours, 7
    long-term *vs.* short-term challenges, 11–12
Toni (global collaboration) case study, 64
transparency, 31–32, 35–36
triggers, emotional, 144–145
trust, vulnerability-based, 107

U

unconscious bias, 136–137, 145
underlying assumptions, 74–75
U.S. News & World Report fact-checking depart-
    ment case study, 1–2, 4–5, 7–8, 14

V

video game example of an achievable challenge, 10
vulnerability-based trust, 107

W

Watson, Kittie W., 52
website redesign example of telegraphing
    change, 20
Weeks, Holly, 45–46
Whitbourne, Susan Krauss, 18
Why Business People Speak Like Idiots (Fugere,
    Hardaway, and Warshawsky), 40
win-win scenarios, 61–62
work hours, increased, 7
workplace bullying
    hostile managers, 18–19
    #MeToo movement, 17
    narcissism's role in, 18
    Sterling Jewelers example of a hostile work
        environment, 17–18

Y

Yates, Kathryn, 33–35

Z

Zuckerberg, Mark, 20–21